The Next Quarter

By Donald Jones

Contents

Introduction

I was 12 years old, and my Uncle Mark and I had just celebrated with a high-five as Ike Hilliard scored his second touchdown of the day. It looked even sweeter in slow motion. As the announcer broke down the play, a vision materialized in my mind: an NFL team (the New York Giants would be preferable, but I wasn't picky) would contact me and ask that coveted question: How would you like to play for our team?

Ten years later, that call came from the Giants, and from the other 31 NFL teams as well. Who would have thought that naïve child's prophecy would turn out to be modest? Most of the teams used the exact words I had imagined while sitting on our couch in Plainfield, New Jersey. Unfortunately, all of them hit me with a follow-up question that had not been part of the original script: Can you first tell us about the drug bust you were involved in last year?

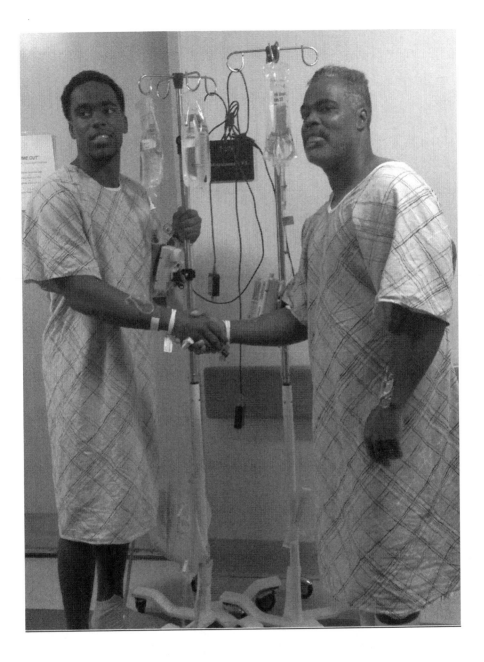

Chapter One

Willing to Bounce Off Bumpers to Make a Play

Even though she couldn't afford them, my mom, Lesley Tyler, a woman with a heavenly smile, athletic body, and philosophical mind, figured out a way to get me new, customized cleats from Eastbay every Christmas in addition to whatever else I asked for. That tradition — which I was always convinced wouldn't happen again the following year, but somehow always did — became the Christmas miracle of my childhood. One of the earliest memories I have, probably because I dust it off so often, is of my mother staying up into the wee hours of Christmas Day wrapping gifts, humming along to the Boyz II Men holiday album. As a workaholic, not by choice, she had the wisdom to enjoy and cherish those moments when it was clear that her sacrifices had paid off.

My mother and I used to race all the time, until I finally beat her in a sprint home when I was 13. If my memory serves me correct, that was the last time she ever challenged me to a footrace.

If I had to pick a favorite pastime with my mom, it would be a less strenuous activity: playing Scrabble. "Come get your butt kicked!" is the invitation she still uses to let me know she just set up the board on the dining-room table. Playing Scrabble with my mom holds a special place in my heart because it's not only about the game. It's about the two of us sitting at the table, mainly focused on the task at hand, but with our discussions ranging from females to football. Those 90-minute battles became extra special to me when I realized that none of my close guy friends had a shared interest in which they regularly partook with their moms. They might go to church, eat at a diner, or occasionally go shopping together, but they didn't experience any true, prolonged mother-son moments. Of course they spoke highly of the women who had brought them into the world, and got into a few childhood fights defending her name, but they hadn't found that common ground, whereas with their dads they spent hours bonding over beer, cars, exercise, sports, women, etc.

I became very scared a few years back when my mother started to call out "Bingo!" while we were playing Scrabble. When I first heard her say that, I thought it was the moment all children dread: when they notice one of their parents slipping away. But when I checked the score sheet and saw that she was whooping me, I had to confront the issue. "Mom, we're playing Scrabble, not Bingo. Why do you keep calling out 'Bingo'?" It hurt to ask, because nobody wants to be the one to break that kind of news to someone. But her response slapped me upside the face. "'Bingo' means I used all seven tiles in one move. Go read the box. I get 50 points for a bingo. And that's 50 points *on top* of the regular points for the word." It turned out Mom was more than all right. I would like to say that she could never beat me, but that would be the furthest from the truth. The truth is that I could never beat her until recently. Now if I get one win, I declare myself the champ and won't give her another game for a while just to enjoy the victory.

I grew up in a rough section of Plainfield, New Jersey, and I knew my mother worked herself to a breaking point for me, so her struggles became mine. She was often stressed about work and financial issues. I often told her, "I'm going to get rich and get us out of here one day. We won't have to worry about anything anymore." My mother never replied to

4

these statements, but she did return a curious "I'm listening" smile that made me feel she was accepting my offer.

When I was five or six, I relocated with my mom to Atlanta, Georgia, to follow her job. This was very hard on me, because all I wanted at that age was to be around my entire family. Plus, everyone I knew who was my age was in New Jersey. It was even harder because, like all kids in split families, I wanted to see my parents get back together.

Despite how young I was, my mother gave me a few opportunities to fly back to New Jersey by myself. With that, I learned very early to be independent. Flight attendants would treat me not as a child, but as a regular passenger, and that worked wonders for my confidence. After some time spent with her, my mom let me move back to New Jersey to be with my father, my Uncle Mark, and my dog. They were bachelors at the time, including the dog, so I knew a different type of learning was about to take place.

My father is a workhorse. Even today, in his late 40s, he hits the gym seven days a week. By "gym," I mean the collection of half-decent throwaways from the YMCA that reside in his garage, and that he and a few of his pals push to the limit. As recently as last week, he challenged me to see who could bench press more. "Feel my arm," he said with a half-serious grin. "I see you looking at me. You know I'm in the gym every day."

Ever since my teenage years, I have been told how much my father and I look alike: long hair, stocky build, and, to pay the man his due, good looks. Before his hair went gray and people started mistaking him for my grandfather, we would occasionally be called twins.

He had his own landscaping business as far back as I can remember. When I was growing up, it was one of the only landscaping businesses in Plainfield that was thriving. My father built it from the ground up, going from a beat-up truck and no trailer to a huge truck and multiple trailers, to which he would later add a large decal showing himself with long hair and his German shepherd. The logo on the side said "Shepherds of Landscaping," and when he drove locally, people would call out his nickname, "The Black Jesus." He had no trailer, just an old pickup truck with ramps, which he used to push heavy equipment onto the truck bed. I grew up seeing my dad as the ultimate businessman, as he expanded his company with multiple trucks and the latest equipment. He started out working on small houses in Plainfield and went on to do commercial properties throughout northern New Jersey. I developed my work ethic by taking note of his. My dad was more of a "let's shake on it" businessman than a "let's put it in writing" one, and people always took him at his word.

My father typically worked seven days a week, and he couldn't always make my games. Still, I always checked the stands for him. Sometimes he wasn't there, and I would be upset, but I knew he was out doing what he had to do so I could be doing what I wanted to do. I always wanted to impress him; I still do. I wanted him to be a part of all my shining moments; I still do.

He took me to various functions where I expanded my horizons. My dad and his buddies were party animals. They looked for any reason to go a little crazy. One of the events we went to every year was the Whitney Young Classic, a football game in the Meadowlands between two black colleges. We took his work truck and trailer and had the ultimate tailgate with the

Green Machine. The whole parking lot partied with us. Of course, we always had a DJ. We sold food to all kinds of people and came home with empty trays. It was another hustle for him. I couldn't get enough of the fried fish and wings, but the pinnacle was always being invited to toss the pigskin with guys twice my age, and holding my own with them. With cars as our sidelines, I was willing to bounce off bumpers to make a play that would make people holler.

Those were the good days. I didn't have a care in the world. There were always groups of bikers who would come and try to show off. My dad's crew came from different worlds, but good food has a way of distracting people from superficial differences. I became a bit infatuated with them. When I got home, still electric from the day, I would put a piece of cardboard above the back tire of my bicycle to make it sound like more a motorcycle, then ride around popping wheelies with the most rugged Harley look I could conjure.

One of the reasons I am so driven and independent today is that my dad made me work with him at a young age. He taught me where true effort could take you. He always had a hustle mentality, which spilled over into me. When I got to a certain age, he made me work for the things I wanted. I hated it at the time, but he was teaching me how to survive in the world. He never wanted me to be pampered and unable to fend for myself. I watched the way he busted his hump for the little he had, and it rubbed off on me.

I was the only child for 11 years, and the only grandchild on my dad's side for about nine. Despite my dad's protests, his parents spoiled me. They bought me anything I asked for and took me anywhere I wanted. My grandparents on my mom's side also showered me with gifts and love. They didn't have much money, but if I asked, they would somehow make it happen.

My mother eventually came back to New Jersey, and I moved back in with her. One of the things she always wanted was for me to keep going to church. I didn't like it very much because I was a hyperactive child who found it hard to follow the monotone lectures. It got to the point where I would fall asleep on purpose. She didn't want to force me to be religious, but to let me discover my relationship with God on my own. Foremost, she wanted me to live right and do right by others. She always put her family and friends first, just as her mom did. "Family first," with family including our closest friends, was the path she hoped I would follow by her example. "Respect and cherish your family," she often reminded me, "because they won't always be here."

I went back and forth between my parents on certain days, including holidays. I had to listen to them argue whenever I went from one to the other. They fought intensely in courtrooms over custody and child support. It took a toll on me. I was always scared they were going to bring me into the courtroom and make me choose where I wanted to live.

My mom moved on and had two more children, my sister Daja and my brother DeAndre. My father remarried and eventually had another son, Taj. From a young age, my brothers and sisters all had their own personalities. Despite our genetic bonds, we couldn't have been more opposite. All I cared about was sports. They loved computers and fashion. I am glad they didn't try to be like me. They weren't afraid to be themselves.

Because I was the only child for so long, I never wanted to be home when I was young. I spent many days at my cousins' place. Jamal, Buddah, and I did everything together. We played sports together. We chased girls together. We got in trouble together. I also had a brother and sister named Hanae and Eddie. My mom and their dad dated for years. They became family. We had our ups and downs, like real brothers and sisters. We fought. We had good times. But we stayed together. I needed them.

My mom could have used being a single mother as an excuse to complain, but she pushed on and did what she had to do. My parents instilled love, hunger, and hustle in me. They showed me the core values I would need to thrive in the world. My mother and father equally helped me construct the foundation I needed to become a man.

My parents did everything they could to raise me the right way despite the circumstances. I thank them for that. My father could have walked away, as so many fathers do. I used to obsess about the stories my friends would tell — how they had no respect for their fathers because they hardly saw them. I couldn't imagine life without my dad. That was when it really sank in for me: Someday my father will be gone. Not that I expected him ever to abandon us, but I realized that he could be taken out of my life at any moment. After that epiphany, I made the transition from obeying my father to respecting my father. That lesson has become one of my favorite, and most controversial, philosophies to impart when I visit schools today: Don't obey any of your teachers, but respect them all. When I release this whopper on the students, I get somewhat dirty looks from the teacher in the room. However, when I wrap things up with a discussion of obedience versus respect, the teachers jump on board, especially after I discuss with the class the few people who respectfully declined the requests from police officers and firefighters to head back inside the burning South Tower on September 11, 2001.

Chapter Two

There Wasn't Exactly a Scholar Steering My Ship

I began playing sports at eight years old. I liked them immediately because they became a tool to gain exposure to new worlds. Right from the start, I loved the notions of being on a team and competing against others, and before long, my whole life was about sports. I tried many, and every time, things just clicked, to the point that it became hard to find a sport I wasn't good at. Some people are natural athletes. Others are not so blessed, so they have to work a little harder just to do some of the things a natural athlete can do with ease.

As early as I can remember, I was told that I was blessed with speed, size, and skill. Despite that, I knew I still had to work hard to separate myself. My father drilled a strong work ethic into me: "Natural talent will only get you so far, because in time, you'll always run into someone better than you," he said. "Plus, once you move up enough levels, you will hit that plateau where everyone has natural talent."

I was introduced to sports at the age of seven. The first sport I was introduced to was baseball. I started out playing tee ball. It was boring. I wanted to be pitched to, to be challenged. I wanted someone at least to underhand the ball to me. I would consistently hit it to the outfield. I was a natural at hitting and fielding. I grasped most of the game right away. For the stuff I didn't get, I watched the pros play on television, and my body just knew what to do the next time I took the field.

I moved up to the minors of the Plainfield Babe Ruth League when I turned eight years old. I played for the Diamondbacks. (I thought it was so cheesy that we were named after professional teams and wore uniforms that resembled theirs. It was obviously a decision made by grown-ups who were less concerned about our playing the sport for fun and more interested in finding a sense of accomplishment through their kids.) We had a stacked team. It really wasn't fair. We would crush our competitors. Everybody on our team had serious skills. The other coaches would always try to say we were cheating. They would come at us with things like, "Their bats are illegal," or, "They're not allowed to throw those pitches." Their coaches and parents were so hostile toward us, you would have thought we were stealing their lunch money on the side.

My last year in the minors, we beat the Rockies in the World Series. It was a crazy competition. They went ahead by a substantial amount in the last game of a three-game series. We came back at the end. It was a very controversial game, because a normal base hit for us turned into a wild play at the plate that went our way.

To some, these kinds of early experiences may seem small or trivial, but for me, they were formative. They gave me a taste of sweet victory that I would never get out of my mind. Once you are a winner at something important in life, you want to be a winner at everything important in life.

In the spring and summertime, all we did was play baseball. We would get a pickup game going and stay on the field for hours. When there weren't enough kids around to fill all the positions, we would move to the side of the field and play "run down." This simulates what many consider to be the toughest situation in baseball: A runner is stuck between bases, and the infield players are tossing the ball back and forth, hoping to wear them down. There are two, three, sometimes four players trying to run you down and tag you out before you reach one of the bases safely. We would do that for hours, and when someone actually eluded a tag and made it to a base, our shouts must have reached the heavens. Sometimes we would go days without someone pulling that off.

On days when we had summer camp, we still went out to play catch, just to stay smooth. My cousin Dashaun and I stayed with my grandmother during the summer. During breakfast, we would always say the same thing: "Catch the football or the baseball?" We would walk to the field around the corner from my grandmother's house. He would pitch to me, and with each swing I would try to take it out of the park. It was he and I at the park in the middle of the day in the summertime. It was pure joy to be out there. If we decided to catch the football, we would play in front of my grandmother's house. We would always try to throw the ball as far as we could. Dashaun had a very strong arm. He would tell me to go to the corner so that he could try to reach me. Since I was the younger cousin, I was always the one who had to run out to the corner. That was how we trained ourselves. We never had any official training. Our families didn't have the money for that. We got better by watching each other, identifying weak areas, and improving on them all the time. We weren't in competition with each other; we genuinely wanted to heighten each other's game. We always imagined ourselves playing in the pros. We talked about what it would be like when we got there and were able to play against each other. I would spend the night at his house, and we would stay up for hours, imagining our names announced to a sold-out stadium with raucous fans wearing our jerseys.

I played for the Diamondbacks in Plainfield's minor league for two years, and then I moved up to the major league and played for the Rays with the same teammates. We could do it all. We stole every base we could. We couldn't take leads off the base while the pitcher wound up, like you see on television. But as soon as the pitch was released — and most of the time, a split second beforehand — we were like sprinters bursting off the starting block. We would take off while the catcher was throwing the ball back to the pitcher. Our speed brought a different element to the game. We also used it on defense to turn the occasional double play, which was unheard-of at our age. We could throw every pitch. We threw curveballs and sinkers. We threw two-seam and four-seam fastballs. We could all hit home runs. We learned it all not from a book or a coach, but from the carefree enjoyment of playing in the streets and parks at twilight. The thug life ceased to exist for us while we were on the field, even though the toughest guys in town played as well. There was a certain respect given to those looking to write their tickets out of town in a legitimate manner. We simply had the love for sports, and it became a sanctuary from the reality most others our age were dealing with on the streets.

When I got to the major league, one of the things I wanted to do was be in the home-run derby. All you had to do was have one home run before the all-star game, and you were in. I grew up watching the older guys "go yard" during the home-run derby. I couldn't wait to participate. When I finally got in, though, all I wound up hitting was one home run. I kept hitting ground balls and pop-ups. I overthought the event, and that took the fun and my heart out of it. I spent way too much time analyzing and made the mistake of letting my mind and body shift from intense to tense. The results spoke for themselves.

The Plainfield traveling teams were always good in the tournaments in our area. The traveling league was made up of the best players in the city. We had to try out, but we knew who would make the team before the coaches did. We had the same team every year. We would travel to the surrounding towns and win a lot of tournaments. People didn't expect us to win because we were young, mostly black kids from the inner city who "had no discipline." They were wrong. Their kids passively obeyed their coaches, while we respected the game. Who do you think had the edge?

On weekends, we would have two or three games a day in different cities. It was a lot for our families, but it brought all of us closer together.

We played in one tournament in Colonia, New Jersey, and I won MVP. I had a few home runs. I also pitched in the last game, and the other teams' coaches complained because I had a mean curve and a sinker. Their players didn't know how to adjust, because they just followed their coaches' orders, and you can't teach a kid to hit a new pitch in the middle of a game.

That said, the coaches didn't know what to do with me. As a kid, I wasn't supposed to have junk pitches like that. The rules stated that we weren't allowed to throw curveballs because we could hurt our arms. We didn't care about the rules. We cared about beating teams that thought they were better than us because they came from a better town.

When I was 13, I started playing on my middle school's team. Middle school wasn't as fun as Little League days, but my friends were there, so I stuck with it. I went on to play in the Amateur Athletic Union, for a team up in Warren, New Jersey. That was my first taste of going out of state for away games. I had a lot of fun on that team. I was one of two black guys on the team, and it was my first time being around affluent families. These kids' parents were doctors, lawyers, and business owners. It was exposure to a completely different world. They got the best training, often from former professional athletes. That was the first time I saw natural talent go up against someone who had the best possible help to build on moderate talent.

Warren is a very high-class town up in the mountains. All the guys on my team came from very rich homes. They had so much money and freedom. I would go to their houses and be amazed at the size and luxury. They were able to do anything they wanted because they had the space. I wanted to live like that. They exposed me to a different life from what I knew.

The biggest highlight of my childhood baseball career was going to Australia and New Zealand at age 15 to play ball. We flew from New Jersey to California, and from there took a 15-hour flight to New Zealand. Our team was made up of guys from all over the United States. It was a blast. I was able to learn from a totally different perspective. I had assumed that they played baseball totally differently over there, but it was all the same. I was able to see famous landmarks that I had never even learned about in school. I got a chance to check out volcanoes, pristine beaches, koalas, and other things we never saw back in the States, like rugby. They even arranged it so we could feed some kangaroos.

Rugby was easy to pick up because I played football back home. I didn't enjoy cricket as much. You can probably guess the first thing that went through my mind when I heard we were going to check out a famous cricket stadium: I had plans to borrow a friend's camera and bring back photos to make my science teacher proud of me. The actual experience was dull, mostly because there was nothing close to grasshoppers there.

Being on the other side of the world as a 15-year-old taught me a lot. There was so much out in the world for me to experience, and that's when I realized sports could be a tool for me to experience what most others would never get a chance to.

I played baseball all the way through high school. But while I was very good at it, it just wasn't my sport. I lost the love for it as I got the older because the practices consisted of drill after drill of fundamentals that many of us had already mastered. I was just good enough to make it through seasons as a starter with a decent year. Pitching got harder the older we got, and because I didn't train like I should have, it was especially hard on me. I still hit home runs and had good games, but I lacked the techniques that could have put me over the top.

My senior year in high school, I had a good season and hit a few home runs. I played well in the field. But I decided to stop mid-season because I wanted to work to raise money for my senior class trip and my senior prom. I got a job at Home Depot. I learned a few things there, but all I really did was drive the forklift. I should have been on the field with my teammates in our last season together. My coach, Mike Passe, was upset with my decision to leave the team. He came to Home Depot and talked with my boss, who agreed to change my schedule so that it wouldn't conflict with practices or games and I could finish out the season.

I was blessed to have a coach like him. Most coaches would have just let me leave. But Mr. Passe was too competitive — plus, he needed me to help the team win. He saw potential in me. He was only 24, which made him good at getting through to us. He played some professional ball, too. He had an arrogant but funny swag about him. His best attribute was his competitive nature. He was hard on us because he wanted to win, but at the same time, he would joke and laugh with us.

One Saturday morning, as I woke up and got ready for a baseball game, my mom noticed a strange hole in the wall next to where she had been sleeping. Then she found similar holes in the front door of the house, as well as in the steps. I knew that the holes looked like bullet holes, but it was strange because I hadn't heard any gunshots.

The holes had us stumped. Maybe they had been there the whole time and we had just never noticed. That theory was debunked when my mother dug a bullet out of the wall.

That was the first and last time I ever held a bullet. We soon learned that there had been a shootout the night before, and a few strays had hit our house. My mom cried, partly from horror and partly from relief. My sister had spent the night out. If she had stayed home, she would probably have been sleeping directly in front of the spot where the bullet hit the wall. I remember my mother sobbing, "If my baby was here, she would be gone right now. She would've been shot in the head. God is so good." Then she kept repeating, "We have to get out of here."

I was late getting to my game, because the police came down and questioned us to see if we knew what had happened. They asked a bunch of us, "Did you hear anything last night?" I had no response, because I had slept through the entire thing. When I got to the field, my coaches looked at me in disbelief as I told them what had happened. I felt as if they didn't know whether to believe me or not. Those types of things could happen at any time living in Plainfield.

Baseball was fun, but if it had been football, I wouldn't have been late that day. I would have found a way to get there on time. As an adult, I sometimes find myself wishing I had stuck with baseball instead, but then I realize my first true love was football, and the heart wants what the heart wants.

I started playing flag football when I was seven years old. I was a little bigger than my teammates, and football, like baseball, came very easily to me. I scored touchdown after touchdown in my Pop Warner days. It got so bad, sometimes the coaches would move me to the offensive or defensive line so that they could hide me and I could immediately affect the outcome of games. During my Mighty Mite days, I wore a jersey with the number 99. I had a neck brace and a single-bar facemask. It was the same mask that our linemen wore. I looked horrible. I played quarterback but looked like a defensive lineman. I hope no photos of me from back then ever pop up.

I started playing for the Plainfield Cardinals football team at age 11. The city had two Pop Warner teams, the Cardinals and the Vikings, and back then, we were fierce rivals. The games were flooded with parents and families from both sides. It would be almost as packed as the high-school games. There was always tension between us. We were all friends and family from the same town, but when it came to those games, a deep line was drawn in the sand. I would torch them every year. I would go for multiple touchdowns, interceptions, and big hits. My friends and I still talk about the time I hit one of their players into the garbage can on the sideline.

(Yeah, I lined him up for it.) The Vikings' coaches wanted me to play for them badly since I was beating them every year. They offered to buy me a pair of Jordan sneakers to switch to their team. Behind my parents' backs, they told me, "We will get you whatever you want if you come play for us."

I had to think about what was more important. All children love new things, and if you are going to buy them, I will take them. I kept thinking about how I could milk this and get whatever I wanted from week to week. I could be so fresh when I went to school. On the other hand, all my best friends were with the Cardinals. That was a tough, not to mention unethical, situation to put someone not quite a teenager in. They offered me more things as I sat on the fence, but I never left the Cardinals. My friends were on the Cardinals, and that made me proud to be a Cardinal. Plus, I wasn't sure if my dad would be pissed or proud when he spotted my new footwear.

Every weekend was the same during football season. We would attend the Plainfield High School games — they were one of the top-ranked teams in the state — and play "free fall" behind the bleachers. (In free fall, one person throws a football in the air, and someone catches it and tries to score. Everyone tries to tackle the person with the ball. It made us so much better, because we had to evade 15 guys for a touchdown. We would play free fall and pretend we were star players from the high-school team or the NFL.) Those games were packed. There was no sitting room. People would crowd around the gates, standing wherever they could find a decent view. But we never watched, because we thought we were better than most of the high-school players, and they ran many of the same plays we did. We were overconfident at that age, but because the cheerleaders gathered around the best players after the game, we realized we could learn something from them after all.

Our Pop Warner games were on Sundays. We even played free fall before those. Our coaches would be pissed, because they didn't want us to wear ourselves out before the actual game. They would come over and say, "If you guys don't go and sit down..." Our parents would sometimes come over to tell us the same thing, but we never listened. We always found a way to sneak off and keep playing. We would play until it was time to weigh in, and then we would line up right next to the other team. It was intimidation time. We would put tape all over our facemasks, trying to look mean. I can't lie — I was intimidated by some of the teams we played, but I tried my best never to give them the satisfaction of seeing it in my eyes. Some of the players always looked big and mean. They put extra thigh pads in their pants to make themselves look bigger. Those were the days.

The current generation of young athletes is not the same as we were growing up. They don't practice like we did. They show up late and only want to scrimmage. They don't go outside and play by themselves. They spend a lot of time in the house, playing video games or on a computer.

Every year, I moved to a new level of Pop Warner, until I eventually reached the top level, called midgets. When I became comfortable there, my father talked me into moving up to the middle-school team. He said it was time to play with the older guys. I had dominated Pop Warner enough. I was scoring two or more touchdowns per game. My father thought that it had become too easy, and that and it was time for me to go to a high level to learn more. "You're not being challenged down there. If you want to excel, you have to play with the big boys," he said. It was hard, because most of my friends still played Pop Warner, but he was right.

The middle-school kids were big, but I got used to it quickly. I played quarterback. My best play was a sneak up the middle. I took a few of them all the way. I couldn't really throw, but I could run faster than Forrest Gump. We ran an option system, which played right into my hands. The quarterback wasn't required to throw the ball much in the option system. I just had to be able to run the ball, hand it off to the running back, or toss it to the running back. I didn't have the strongest arm, but I could run and score touchdowns, which was what I wanted to do anyway.

After middle school, I went on to freshman ball. It didn't take long for the coaches to move me up to see if I could handle varsity. I didn't get a chance to play in any varsity games that first season, but it was fun just to be in the locker room and on the sidelines with the guys. I learned a lot during the varsity games, and I used those lessons to shine during the freshman games, which were at different times.

As a sophomore, I got a lot of playing time in varsity games. We had a great team, with a bunch of guys who went on to play at top colleges, including Eugene Monroe, who wound up being taken in the first round of the NFL draft in 2009. We had the potential to win the whole state tournament, but we didn't even get past the first round of the playoffs. The competition in our division was tough. We played a lot of inner-city teams, which were very talented but lacked discipline. But when we played teams that weren't from the inner city, they would beat us. They had more discipline, and we lacked coaching. Our coaches didn't know how to work with us as individuals, and it came back to haunt us in the playoffs.

My junior year was bad. We had a lot of talent, but we only won a couple of games. We lost to teams we had no business losing to. To make things worse, our coach was suspended because of a fight that us players got into. It happened after a bad loss on a Friday night. When we got back to our field, there were some random guys smoking behind the field house. Our coach told us to make sure they didn't leave until he had checked whether anything had been stolen. When a few of us went to question them, a fight broke out. Two of the guys were injured very badly, and they claimed that our coach had told us to beat them up. The year went from bad to worse that Friday and just kept unraveling.

We dealt with many issues in the inner city, on and off the field. Looking back, some of it was ridiculously funny. Some things you just don't expect to happen during a football game. For instance, during my junior year, one of our wide receivers was hurt on a play. Our quarterback, Jay, could also play wide receiver, so he filled in, and our backup quarterback, Nadir, replaced him. Nadir came into the game and called a play in the huddle. Jay moved out to the receiver position next to me, in the slot on the left side of the field. We approached the line of scrimmage, and Nadir got under center to snap the ball. Then he had a change of heart. He looked out to Jay and said, "Jay, I can't throw to my left." The other team's defense looked like they weren't buying our ruse, but the sad truth was that we were as lost as we looked. We only had maybe 15 seconds on the play clock, so we had to move fast. You could see in Jay's eyes that he wanted to shrug Nadir off, but they quickly swapped places, and then Nadir shouted, "Man, snap the damn ball and throw it!" Jay called for the snap, awkwardly tossed it to the left, and got picked off.

We laugh about that to this day, but it was really indicative of the types of things we had to deal with. We had the talent. We just didn't have the coaching, which meant that we didn't have a chance.

Come junior and senior years, recruiters didn't come to me. Our coaches never helped us get into college. Coming from Plainfield High School, we didn't get much recognition, even though we had vast amounts of talent. We didn't know about the various football camps or combines. We didn't know about the all-important Rivals.com, which was a great way for college coaches to find the best high-school players around the country. The site would rank players based on their high-school film or how they performed at the combines. I was forced to make calls to college coaches myself. My teammates and I would get together to make our own highlight tapes. We would connect two VCRs and copy the tapes. Our film had lines through the middle; the resolution was horrible. But it was obvious that our coaches weren't going to lift a finger. We even had to mail the tapes out ourselves. The school did absolutely nothing to help us get into good colleges, but when anyone from the team did, the school advertised the accomplishment as if it had made it happen.

Because we didn't get the recognition we deserved, I was never a five-star athlete on any of the recruiting websites. I don't think I had any stars for most of my high-school career. So I wasn't on colleges' radar, even though everyone who mattered in New Jersey football knew my name. I would look on the Rivals site and think to myself, *these guys are not that good. Why can't I get on there? I'm better than them.*

There was only one person who helped me get the recognition I felt I deserved — only one person who went the extra mile for the football players with higher aspirations. He was the athletic trainer at Plainfield High School, Frank Colabella, and he was a blessing to us. He took us to numerous events to try to get us exposure. He drove us in a church van to football camps as far away as Maryland and Virginia. He would get as many guys as he could to go, sometimes 10 of us. There were times the van broke down on the highway and we had to wait for it to be fixed or hope a ride would come get us. It was fun and business at the same time. We just wanted to get out of the inner city to check out the best talent around.

Mr. Colabella didn't get anything out of it. He did it out of the kindness of his heart, and yet people didn't trust him because he was a white guy helping black teenagers in a black community. He had a family back home that he was missing time with in order to give us more exposure. We wouldn't have known anything about college combines or football camps if it hadn't been for him. He didn't care where the event was. He would take us, because nobody else had a clue.

My friend Rasoul and I went to the U.S. Army National Combine in San Antonio, Texas. Only the top players in the country attended this combine, and Frank flew there with us with no complaints. Going to these events opened my eyes to the talent that was out there. Before, I thought I was the man and believed that I was untouchable, but once I got to these events and saw guys from different states, I received a much-needed reality check that let me know how good I wasn't. It offered me a new perspective on my competition for college scholarships. These guys were good. Most of them were from warmer climates and could play year-round. In New Jersey, most of the guys I played with went cold turkey on the gym starting around November, and their bodies quickly fell out of shape, as if they were intentionally adding extra layers of fat for the winter.

That exposure was great for me and is great for all children. It gave me something to work for. It made me realize how much time I needed to put in if I wanted to compete at the top level. Without Mr. Colabella, I wouldn't have gotten that push. Our parents had no idea these events even existed before he put them on their radar. He set up seven-on-seven games against other high schools in the state so we could get some experience against real talent.

But the people of Plainfield didn't appreciate what Mr. Colabella was doing, simply because he was white. They did everything they could to get him fired. They even tried to get me to testify against him. They brought me into the field house one day and showed me documents stating that what he was doing was illegal. They had receipts as proof of all the events we had attended. "Look at these documents," they said. "Do you know that what he is doing is illegal?" I am not sure how they got the documents. The only thing I could think was that they had talked to someone who went with us and gotten him to play both sides of the fence. They tried to get me to flip. "If we bring you in to testify, will you speak up?" I wanted the exposure Mr. Colabella was giving us, so I wasn't going to testify against him. Plus, he had earned our respect, so none of us said a word. All I wanted to do was compete against the most skilled players so that I could get my name out there and earn a scholarship, and Mr. Colabella was the only person in the town who was doing that for us. But they eventually came up with a reason (unknown to me) to push him out, as they did many just like him.

My senior year finally arrived. It was my time to shine. I felt it was my team because I had been named captain. We won a good number of games and went into the playoffs strong. But in the first round of the playoffs against Union High School, we got beaten very badly. We were outcoached that day; they made adjustments at halftime and we didn't. They had a running back who ran through us the second half. It was like he transformed along with his coaches' play calling. We had beaten Union early in the season. It's difficult to beat a team twice, and we found that out the hard way.

Still, I finished that season with over 1,000 yards receiving. I made the All-County, All-Conference, and All-State teams.

During my senior year, I went on a few college visits, some official and others unofficial. Coaches can only invite players for official visits if they have offered them a scholarship or plan on offering one. Temple University had already offered me a full ride, so they were my first visit. The coaches took us and our families to see the stadiums, and we went out to dinner with them every night. Later on, we went out by ourselves with guys from the team. They got us drunk before taking us to parties. My host took me to meet several attractive women he knew. He took me to the liquor store to buy booze for the after-parties, and to a crack house to buy marijuana. At first I thought to myself, *if the coaches find out what we're doing, we'll be kicked off the team and arrested.* Then it occurred to me that someone had to have put my host up to it and picked up the tab. I didn't care either way, because I was having fun. I had no reason to say anything.

The summer after my senior year, I was nominated for the New Jersey Top 100 team and was invited to play in the North-South Game at

Rutgers University, home of the very first college football game. The North-South Game was great to play in, but it wasn't the top competition. Everyone wanted to play in the Governor's Bowl, which was New Jersey vs. New York. You had to be going to a Division 1 college in order to be invited to that game. I didn't get that invite because I had lost out on all of my D1 scholarships.

I wanted to take my frustrations out on everyone in the North-South Game, and I ended up the MVP of the game. I went over 100 yards and scored a sweet touchdown. They ran the same play to me over and over. It was a reverse to me, and it worked every time. It was the final stamp on a great high-school career and a huge stepping-stone to college. It was also the first time I could really see that I was among the best in the state and even the nation.

All of that might have meant something if I could have accepted any of the countless scholarship offers I was receiving. The Temple visit was amazing, and of course I wanted to go there, but I couldn't get through the NCAA Clearinghouse. Unfortunately, there wasn't exactly a scholar steering my ship at the time.

Chapter Three

How a Monster Is Created

Possibly the biggest conundrum in inner cities is the education system. Growing up, everyone in my town would hear that the city was focused on making its school system better. We never saw it. Many of us noticed that those promises arose at the same time every year and disappeared right after Election Day.

Our test scores are consistently at the bottom of the rankings in New Jersey. Every day, more kids fall through the cracks, and I often wonder if it's more the teachers' fault or the parents'.

Most people would agree that there are several reasons the children of the inner city communities are not doing as well as those in surrounding towns. I believe that the first problem is their parents, many of whom are not educated enough to teach their children anything but hustling. Most parents preach the importance of going to college, but they don't know anything about the process of getting into one. In fact, I would say they know about as much about getting into college as they do about getting into professional sports: little to nothing. But maybe we shouldn't blame the victims. With millions of city tax dollars going to Plainfield's schools every year, the average person might expect that the leaders of the school district are doing what is in the best interest of our youth — but that is rarely the case. One of the most shocking discussions I've ever had about schools was with a friend who is a teacher. He said, "Schools today are not created with the student's best interest in mind." And this man was his school's Teacher of the Year.

Our parents need to be more savvy, and that process could begin with an easy step: attending one of the monthly Board of Education meetings in their city, which are open to the public and typically have an open microphone session where parents can voice their concerns and frustrations. Most cities televise these meetings on a local channel, so chances are that one of the elected Board of Education members will address such criticisms.

It's hard for parents to make a convincing argument for going to college when they never went themselves. Many are okay with their children saying, "College isn't for everyone." That is a lazy way of saying, "I don't feel like doing all that work right now." We need to set the bar higher for our children. If we keep raising our expectations, generations of families will come out of poverty. Stop the rising tide of mediocrity. The cycle has to end somewhere, and if parents won't do it, it's on other people in the town to step in.

The next problem in Plainfield, and in many cities like it, is politics. The people in power are not doing the right things to make sure our children have the best. They are more worried about making a name or money for themselves. We constantly hear stories about people at the top stealing money or engaging in other illegal activities. Our youth should always be the priority.

We don't have teachers in place who make it about the kids. When I was in school, we always had new teachers just looking to put something on their résumés and leave, or veterans who watched the clock and gave us busywork. We had very few textbooks, and those we did have were missing key pages that students had ripped out. Some didn't even have covers. Most of the books were older than we were, and the maps showed countries that no longer existed. We couldn't take the books home because there weren't enough of them, so we had to take copious notes during the school day in order to do our homework. It is very hard to learn from a book that has pages missing or profanity scribbled throughout. How are students supposed to take math problems seriously when there are naked stick figures next to them?

Then there are the guidance counselors, who should play a big role in students' lives. They should be pushing students to take the right tests, to prepare with practice exams, and to receive any necessary tutoring. The vast majority of parents in our communities know very little about the ins and outs of college applications, academic requirements, and financial aid. Counselors and teachers should be the parents away from home.

I barely saw my guidance counselor. I didn't even know who she was until my senior year, when I failed the math portion of the HSPA test, which we had to pass to graduate, by two points. I went to see her to find out my scores, and she chuckled as she read them to me. She then told me, "You just have to pass this SRA class to graduate." (SRA was a class that we had to pass in order to graduate high school if we couldn't pass the HSPA test.) A student should not be meeting his guidance counselor for the first time during his senior year of high school. At a minimum, she should have made it her business to meet me, and everyone else on her roster, at least once a year. Is that asking too much? We also should have had an academic advisor assigned specifically to make sure us athletes were on track.

When I was very young, I was an exemplary student. I always had straight A's and B's on my elementary school report cards. At Woodland and Cedar Brook Elementary Schools, I was fortunate to have some great teachers who went the extra mile for us. My favorite teacher of all time was Mrs. Smallwood in fifth grade. She genuinely cared about us. She did more with less to make sure we learned what we would need to be prepared for the next levels of school and life. She didn't mess around with us, either. She kept on us about our grades and pushed us to overachieve, always reminding us that it would get much harder once we got out into the world. She tried to give us a foundation of hard work and consistency to live by.

But when I moved up to Hubbard Middle School, I started to slack off. I got C's for the first time in my life. In my mind, that was the worst thing in the world. I felt as if I had failed the class. I am glad I felt that way. But I didn't use that shame as motivation to get back on track. Instead, my performance got worse and worse as the years went by. I started to cut class. Surprisingly, I got away with it — so I kept doing it. I began hanging out with guys who were known troublemakers in and out of school. I would skip class to visit different lunch periods or throw a football around. I would run through the halls with girls and leave school to go to their houses. Instead of being in a classroom, I would be in a closet with my girlfriend or some other girl.

One day, I cut a class for which my coach was the substitute teacher. He made me do laps that day when I got to practice. He told me if he heard I was cutting class again, he would tell my mom and release me from the basketball team. I didn't want to be kicked off the team, so I slowed down on cutting class — that is, until I got to high school.

I had a lot of fun at Plainfield High School, maybe too much. I had so much fun that it hurt me in the long run. My first two years there are a blur now. I hardly remember being in class, and I can only remember one or two teachers' names. I didn't do any schoolwork. I would come home after practice and my parents would say, "Where is your homework?" I would reply, "I don't have any," or, "I did it in class." I cut class all the time. My only priorities were chasing girls and playing football. I roamed the hallways, and when I saw adults who knew I was supposed to be in class, they literally looked the other way.

When I did attend class, I would sleep or chat with someone next to me. One class that sticks out is a history class I had during my freshman year. The main teacher was out for the marking period. In my high school, having a substitute teacher meant that we could relax and do whatever we wanted to do. I always sat in the back with my headphones on. The first time I did that, I was ready with an "I'm really not feeling well" excuse. But since many of the teachers didn't say anything, it became a habit, and I felt a sense of relief because I had pulled one over on them. I remember saying to myself, "This is going to be a good semester." By the end of the year, I was feeling cocky from being able to turn off class and just listen to my music. I even leaned over to one of my friends and said, "This substitute can't handle this class. I will run this class," just to rub it in that I was the one with the power. I usually did things just to get the class to laugh, or to impress girls.

I didn't take the classes I should have taken to prepare myself for college. Instead, I took classes like auto body or cooking. I took classes that older players told me I could blow off and still get the D I needed to stay eligible to play sports. We never did anything academic in those classes. In auto body, we would be on the computers the entire time, listening to rap battles or watching football highlights. Guys would have rap battles of their own. We would talk about the crime that had happened the night before. We never even did any work on the cars. We didn't have the tools we needed to do any work on the cars. We had three cars in the classroom that had been there for years. Our teacher didn't care. His looked at his newspaper more than at us.

My coach never talked to me about my grades or the classes I was taking. Sometimes I would cut class and visit his room; he was a gym and weight-lifting teacher. We would talk about the team we were playing the next week or what had happened in practice the day before. The assistant coaches would go to his room, too, so I always wanted to be there. They made sure I stayed eligible to play, but nothing more. They never sat me down to tell me I needed to pick my grades up. I was one of the top athletes in the school, so I got away with more than most. I remember getting a lot of warnings, but never anything worse. People always gave me things or passed me through because they thought I would become famous. That is how a monster is created.

My friends had early dismissal because they were seniors, and I would sit by the window to keep an eye out for them as they left. When I saw them at the corner, I would give a shout out the window, and they would wait for me. Since I couldn't leave through the front door, I would climb out of the window in the middle of class while the teacher was talking to a colleague in the hallway. He never said anything to me. I kept doing it because it became a habit, and because I loved catching the look on other students' faces — I thought I was impressing them. And the teacher still gave me a good grade, probably because I didn't bother anyone.

The security guards would let us leave as long we brought them back something to eat. We took full advantage of that, as all of the eateries were right up the street. As we left, they would say to one another, loud enough for us to hear, "I'm really in the mood for some pepperoni pizza," or, "It's been a while since I've had some General Tso's chicken." We would leave school, get something, and come back. Typically, we would drop their food off with them and then leave for good. The guards never wanted to do anything. They didn't care what we did as long as they didn't have to move.

I also had fun outside of school. My friends and I began to drink and smoke pot, which affected me both in class and on the field. We did it because we were the top dogs, and when you hold that spot, you'll do anything to keep it. There was a time back in middle school when eight of us, girls and boys, got drunk during spring break behind the school building. We put crazy amounts of various types of alcohol into water bottles and splashed in some Kool-Aid to make it less conspicuous. It had an expired-medicine taste, but we didn't care, because we wanted to be cool and rule. The girls threw up and passed out in the grass, probably because it was a hot day and we didn't know what we were mixing. My best friend passed out as well. He was so intoxicated that we had to ride him home like a dead weight on the handlebars of a bicycle. We never stopped to think about how we could have gotten ourselves arrested or landed in the hospital. We never stopped to think about how drinking could affect all of us as athletes.

One might expect that debacle to have slowed us down, but we just took things a step further: We started drinking during school hours. My cousin and I would steal liquor from his grandfather and bring it to school in water bottles, and we would drink it between classes. Sometimes we would drink before homeroom and be buzzed first thing in the morning. Other times we would drink or smoke between the two buildings of the high school while everyone else was in class. We didn't care about the consequences if we were caught, because we were invincible.

I couldn't get through games to the best of my abilities because of my new smoking habit. I smoked Black & Milds along with pot. I lost a lot of my stamina — I wasn't really the fastest guy to begin with, and smoking took its toll. I looked very slow on film because I was out of wind after running 20 yards. I would get caught from behind after breaking free on long runs. It made college coaches question my speed and whether they wanted to offer me scholarships.

Our high-school coaches never taught us about the benefits of a proper diet or of staying away from drinking or drugs — not that it would have mattered. A proper diet could have given me a big edge and caught more recruiters' eyes, but my head was in the clouds.

I always thought I could get by just because I was good at sports, because nobody ever pulled me aside and told me otherwise. As a junior in high school, I started to receive letters from major universities. I had decent grades in my electives, but my core GPA was 2.0, which meant straight C's. I didn't have bad grades because I couldn't handle the work; I had bad grades because I didn't take education seriously. It was because I was lazy and worrying about the wrong things.

As I got older, I started to see the consequences. The first thing college coaches ask for when they visit is your transcript. A coach from the

University of Illinois took a look at mine and shook his head. He said, "Where the hell do you think you're going with these grades?" Then he paused, perhaps to let the sting linger. "To be honest," he continued, "you can probably play college ball somewhere, but you won't be going anywhere you've ever heard of with grades like these."

I had multiple college coaches say the same thing to me. They were trying to be honest, hoping that it wasn't too late and that maybe they could wake me up. But my grades were a reflection of my work ethic at the time. I wasn't ready for college because I wasn't ready to work, in the classroom or on the field. I wouldn't have made it through one semester of college with that mindset. And there wasn't a coach anywhere in the country at the D-1 level who would take a chance on me anyway. There were thousands of other players out there who had comparable talent. The coaches could go to the town right next to mine and find someone who was a better investment, as inner cities in the area put out multiple D-1 athletes every year. I didn't see college sports as the business it is. Coaches have a job to do and keep, so why would they take a chance on a kid with skill on the field but nowhere else? I had to be the total package.

I tried to fix things, but it was too late. Once I had let my core GPA drop, it was hard to get it back up. It goes down easily, but improving it is a different story.

Various big-time D-1A coaches did call me. I received hundreds of letters. I went to a combine my junior year, and I was one of the best receivers there. A coach from the University of Wisconsin came up to me and offered me a full scholarship on the spot. (The coaches weren't supposed to talk to us, but I guess he didn't care about the rules; he was looking for whatever advantage he could find.) I was ecstatic. I immediately called home and told my parents. They were just as excited as I was as I recounted what the coach had said to me.

I received a few scholarship offers like that my junior year, but I couldn't get through the NCAA Clearinghouse. The NCAA has a sliding-scale system based on GPA, SAT and ACT scores: If you have a higher GPA, you don't have to score as well on the SAT or ACT, and vice versa. My GPA was 2.0, so I had to score extremely well on the SAT. I scored an 850.

I remember sitting in the examination room, thinking I wasn't going anywhere because the test was so difficult. Everything on it looked foreign to me. I remember looking around at everyone else, wondering if it was as hard for them. I watched the clock tick down fast.

My friend and I were in the same position. We both had offers on the table but couldn't get the SAT scores we needed to make up for our lousy grades. We signed up for extra help, asking teachers around the school how and where we could find the best tutors before taking the test again. Nothing worked.

I was heartbroken. I lost out on hundreds of thousands of dollars in scholarship money. I was beyond embarrassed when I told my parents we would have to pay for school. They were so disappointed. My mom looked at me and said, "I wish there was another way, but you will have to pay for college, not me."

I never thought I would go to a junior college; students in my school were embarrassed when people found out they hadn't made it into a four-year university. I thought if I had to go to a junior college, it should at least be for free. I was wrong. Lackawanna College put me on a partial scholarship my first year, which only covered my room and board. My parents were pissed, and I was forced to take out thousands of dollars in loans.

I had nobody to blame but myself. I had consistently made bad choices during my teenage years, and now they had finally caught up with me. I had wanted to show off for women and be cool. I had wanted to fit into crowds that had nothing going for them. The whole time, I was trying to impress people who really wanted to be like me. They wished they had the talent I had. They wished they had the opportunity I had to get out of our town. But I felt as if what I was doing was corny. I felt that, as a star athlete, I had to act tough or be the class clown. It wasn't cool to go to class if you were a guy. It was lame to be smart if you were a guy. I wanted to be popular. I didn't understand that I already was.

That was when another lesson sank in. If it hadn't been for the gorgeous women at my school, I wouldn't have shown up to a single class. But for all the time I spent checking them out, I missed the obvious: They partied as much as I did, but they were on the honor roll. Whether it was because they were better at multitasking or because they matured about two years faster than the average guy their age, they figured out the system and lived the best of both worlds.

I didn't want people to call me a geek. If you talked proper, people would say, "You talk like a white boy." If you did all your work or a little extra, people called you a teacher's pet. That was the high-school mentality, and I didn't want to be talked about. I wanted to be the popular guy. Even though my sights were on college, it felt as if high school were forever, so that was where I got anchored. And the whole time, I was trying to impress people who wanted to be just like me.

Chapter Four

Take a Small Step Against the Tide of Ignorance

Regular exposure to new ideas and new situations is the key to the development of a successful child. I knew what a better life would be like because sports offered me glimpses of the world outside the inner city. But my friends at the time didn't realize that most of the world was nothing like Plainfield. Heck, most of New Jersey is nothing like Plainfield. Since many of my friends had never traveled outside state borders, the only view they got of the bigger picture was what they saw on television. And the message they received from the boob tube was that being an actor, athlete, or singer was the only way to make it out of poverty.

Unfortunately, this pipe dream is reinforced in many of the classrooms I visit today, where a majority of posted projects on African-Americans and Latinos are about people like Jackie Robinson, Jennifer Lopez, Neymar, and Rihanna. Don't get me wrong; these people have amazing life stories and have served as role models to millions of discouraged teens. But when teachers allow students to use valuable class time to research people whom they already know plenty about, and whom they could easily learn more about during their free time, they are reinforcing the message that if you are African-American or Latino, your best bet is to go the entertainment route.

To prove my point, I will challenge you to the same one-question test — my "Green Quiz," about the bravest teenager in 20th-century United

States history — that inevitably stumps all of the students when I visit a classroom: Who is Ernest Green?

I'll give you a few clues: He is African-American. He is not famous for being an actor, athlete, or singer. His name was probably never mentioned in any of your history classes, so it's not your fault if you can't answer the question either. But you are in luck, because Disney made a movie about him, *The Ernest Green Story*, and now you can take a small step against the tide of ignorance and make sure the middle- and high-school-aged children in your life don't go another week without knowing about this great American hero. Of course, I would rather they also read about his eight peers from Arkansas, which is why you are going to give those lucky children copies of the book *Warriors Don't Cry*, by Melba Pattillo Beals, after they watch the movie — because you will have created a spark inside them, and I guarantee that they will be thirsty for more information about the Little Rock Nine.

In high school, my father and I no longer saw eye to eye. He claimed that he wanted to teach me how to be an independent man, but I didn't like what he was trying to do. He made me work for everything. He wanted me to come help him and his landscaping business during the summers, but I didn't want to work with him all day, every day. I wanted things like a new phone, sneakers, and a car — stuff my friends' pops were buying for them without the hassle. He also had different rules in his house, which I hated. I had lived with my mom for most of my life, until she moved to South Carolina my senior year of high school, and she didn't have half the rules my dad had. She would let me stay in my room with the door closed. He would say, "Ain't no closed doors in my house." There were times I would come into the house and go straight to my room and not say anything to him. He hated that so much that he would come into my room and start yelling at me. He would get even madder when I didn't back down, because I was showing him that I wasn't scared. We didn't start to get along again until after I left for college.

Music, hip-hop in particular, has a huge impact on inner cities. My mother would always say to me, "If you knew your homework like you know those songs, you would be an A student." I listened to music all the time when I was young, and not always the best music. I memorized everything that I listened to. My moods changed depending on what I was listening to, and I wasn't the only one. Music has changed the way we think in the inner city, and it has caused a lot of violence in the process. Lyrics today are pathetic. Students are surprised to hear that I cannot stand Lil Wayne's music. To which I reply: If you have real musical talent, you don't need to go the obvious route of sex, drugs, and violence.

Violence is a big part of why teachers and administrators in places like Plainfield are the way they are. It is a big part of why we can't get good teachers in tough schools. They don't want to deal with disruptive children. Some fear that their students might hurt them. Many of my teacher friends admit to crying at least once a year from the stress of the job. It isn't surprising that the average teaching career, according to the National Education Association, is even shorter than the average professional football career.

One day, a coach from Rutgers University came in to meet with me during my senior year. We sat in the lunchroom and talked about my grades and what I had to do to be admitted. We talked about how good I was on the field and why the coach wanted me. While we were talking, a fight broke out between two girls. It quickly escalated to a crowd of girls and a big riot. The coach and I had to duck carrots and peas on our way out of the cafeteria. He looked at me and ended the conversation there.

In high school, it seemed the focus was more on the pervasive violence than on our education. There were always at least three cops patrolling the school, along with a big group of security guards, though they hardly did anything. To get into the building, we had to walk through metal detectors. The bizarre thing was that nobody stopped people when the detectors went off. They couldn't check everyone every day because it would take too long for us to get into the building. People knew they weren't really checking us, and they took advantage of that. Girls came to school with blades hidden in their bras. Guys carried knives or guns in their bags. It was as if the administrators had just placed the detectors there to create an illusion that the school was a safe place.

If something major had happened in town the day before, or if the administrators got word that something was going to happen, security changed drastically. They stopped everyone and searched everything. They went through our bags thoroughly. They patted us down slowly. If the detectors went off, they searched us again. They had security wands that they used to leave no place unchecked. Getting into the school building became like going through airport security. We sometimes wouldn't get to class until after noon, but that didn't bother the administrators, because they still got credit for a full day. We would sit in our cars in the parking lot, talking and listening to music until we could get in. Sometimes we would leave, get something to eat, and then come back.

My son will never attend a school where metal detectors welcome him at the entrance. I would feel like a failure if he ever had to do that. My son is only three years old, but he knows for damn sure what it means when you enter a place where you have to walk through a scanner. In Malcolm X's words, "by any means necessary" I will make sure that my son can go to school to learn and socialize, without a trace of fear. Raising a child in a situation where he is tense or anxious almost every day will lead to major issues down the road.

One day I caught the New Jersey Transit bus to school to find everyone looking somber. When we got off, the whole school was still in the parking lot, and I knew something was wrong. My cousin Jamal informed me that our friend Leo had been shot in the head by his own cousin earlier that morning.

Leo was only one of many friends who were murdered in their teens. More people were shot mistakenly than the ones the bullets were intended for. When our friends were murdered, we would spend the next school day going to speak to our guidance counselors and the doctors they brought in. We would have a full day of sorrow. Imagine trying to focus on academics while going through that on a regular basis.

Psychologists like to say that the "appreciating consequences" part of the brain isn't fully formed in teenagers, and that is part of the problem, but I believe teen violence has much deeper roots. So many of our youth have no care for their own lives, let alone someone else's. They see no light at the end of the tunnel. Many don't even see the tunnel. They don't see a way of getting out of poverty. So everything becomes about day-to-day survival, and the only way to survive when you have no hope is by living the street life. You feel as if you always have to protect yourself or play a tough role, because that is the way of the inner cities.

New Jersey has a large gang population, which probably has something to do with the fact that it has the highest population density in the United States. We have a lot of street gangs in Plainfield: the Bloods, the Crips, and Latino gangs as well. The gangs are able to recruit with ease because children think joining will make them more popular. They think it's the way to gain respect and get people to have their back.

One year, there was a huge fight between two gangs, Clinton Avenue and the Latin Kings. Guys from Clinton Avenue used a golf club to beat up a Latin King right in front of the school. Most of us, including the teachers, stood there and watched as they beat this guy within an inch of his life. All of the students watching took off running once they heard the police sirens. The next day, there were Latin Kings throughout the school trying to exact revenge, waiting on anyone wearing Clinton Avenue colors. It was scary seeing them. Nothing more ever came of it, but the next couple of weeks were tense. And things like that happened all the time.

When I was in middle school, everyone fought. If two people had a problem, they would fight it out one on one — with a large crowd nearby, of course. As I got older, it turned into jumping people. Have you ever seen 20 people jump someone? There's nothing normal about it. Twenty people punching and kicking one dude — some looking serious, but most with twisted grins on their faces — until he is unconscious and nearly dead. From there, things evolved into gunplay. The street thugs came to consider fighting beneath them. If someone beat up a peer in school or on the streets, he had to start looking over his shoulder, because the person he had fought was bound to come back shooting. He had to shoot back, or he would be shamed and ridiculed to no end. Reputations were the main currency on the street. Every one of us could name certain people whom nobody messed with, because you would not live to see another day if you did.

In the mid-20th century, the psychologist Abraham Maslow developed a pyramid chart titled "Hierarchy of Needs." It states that if a person cannot secure the basic needs of food, safety, and rest, then he will not be able to focus on the loftier needs of accomplishment and reaching his potential. When a teenager has to witness violence every day, how can he truly focus on school and try to better himself? Who can be bothered with report cards while always looking over his shoulder? Who can learn the proper tools necessary to lead a successful life when they are not being taught the proper tools, or guided in the right direction?

Then again, people will look for any excuse not to work hard. It is easy to say, "It's hard to get out of here. This system is designed for us to fail." But anybody can make it out. People with even more on their plates have made it out before you. It is a choice to remain uneducated. It is a choice to be mediocre. And it is a choice that you will live with forever.

After high-school parties, we would go to a 24-hour chicken shack called The Diner. From time to time, people would get shot late at night, but we had to show our faces there, or people would think we were weak. There would be hundreds of us out there until one or two in the morning.

Any time Plainfield had an event, there was always fear of a fight or of gunshots ringing out. The police had to monitor certain people and groups. Some people went to these gatherings just to start fights. (If you can't create, you destroy.) The girls were just as bad as the guys, maybe

47

worse. I saw women dragged from beneath cars where they were hiding, then punched and kicked by multiple assailants until they were unconscious. Girls' faces were slashed with blades. They would purposely wear angular jewelry to mess another girl's face up. It makes me sick to my stomach to think how we must have seemed like savages. We were only living in the moment, and that was normal. But now I fear we may have passed it down.

I was headed down a path of destruction, and my family had no idea. They thought I was the best kid ever. Everyone in town thought I was the best kid, because I could put on an act and charm people. The face I presented bore no resemblance to the actions I took. You could say that I wasn't walking like I was talking. I wasn't a bad kid. I just didn't have the character to do the right things when nobody was paying attention.

I saw the parents of murdered friends break down in tears as they watched their sons and daughters buried. My mother told me multiple times that she had dreams in which I was killed. It wasn't because I was running the streets; it was because of where we lived. I wanted to go to the corner stores all the time and just stand out there with the guys to look cool. Anything could have happened to me, and I wouldn't have had anything to do with it. I said I wanted to make it to the NFL. I said I wanted to provide a better life for my family. But I wasn't doing the right things to make it happen.

Relatives who were around my age were in and out of jail. We never had a family function in which the whole family was there. I wanted to be cool, but I never wanted to end up like them. They did things that would make you scratch your head. I would walk into my grandmother's house and my cousin would be sitting on the couch, playing with guns. He would take them apart and put them back together as if he were trying to impress his drill sergeant. In my eyes at the time, it wasn't bad to be messing with guns; I felt as if I needed to know more about them to be safe on the streets. (Yes, now I realize just how stupid that idea is.) It was the *type* of guns he had that scared me — he had guns people just shouldn't have on the streets. He had many handguns, which were normal to see, but he also had big assault rifles and machine guns. These were guns that you usually only saw on TV or in war.

Guns weren't the only things he was into. He was also into drugs. Sometimes he would tell me to come into the basement with him as he cut or bagged his drugs. I would sit and watch him cut cocaine up, weigh each piece, and bag them on top of the washer and dryer. My grandmother would walk in and scream at him at the top of her lungs to get that stuff out of her house. She never stopped him from coming, though, because she was just that type of woman. She could never turn away people who needed help, even if they didn't yet realize they needed help.

There were times when the cops saw me in front of my house, rushed up, and handcuffed me, mistaking me for my cousin. When they figured out I wasn't him, they began questioning me to see if I might slip and say something of value to them. But the interrogation was typically short. "Where is he?" "I don't know." They would harass me for 15 minutes in cuffs and then just let me go. It was humiliating.

My family robbed people. They sold drugs. They shot at people. Most of these things they did in front of my grandmother's house. I learned a lot from sitting on that stoop. I learned about the lifestyle they lived: They had to look over their shoulders wherever they went. Every time they

49

stepped out the door, they felt as if they were being watched. They always told me about prison and what it was like. They would say things like, "Don't ever end up like us. You're a strong guy, but you don't want to end up in jail. You are better than that." The contrast between hanging out with them and with my uncles and father, who were businessmen, taught me what I should be doing and what I shouldn't. It really took a village to raise me. I had to make my mistakes in life before I realized that I was wasting my time and talent. It really started to bother me that the police knew me on a first-name basis.

Popularity is a disease. It starts at a very young age and doesn't end for some of us until we are well into adulthood. I put so much energy into being the best looking and most popular that I neglected to pursue my dreams the right way. I wanted to fit into crowds I had no business being around. I didn't realize that I already had the golden ticket in my hands.

It takes a strong person to stand out and go after his goals. It takes sacrifice, but there are oceans of opportunities that stretch far beyond what you can see. It comes down to one question: Do you want to be remembered for what you did in high school or what you did after high school?

Part of me wishes that I could have my middle- and high-school years back to do over. Cutting class and chasing girls took me further from my dreams. My cousins were in gangs, and I wanted to be like them. Little did I know that they wanted to be like me — an irony realized too late. I don't fault them; they were products of their environment. Nor do I blame my teachers, a few of whom I probably made go prematurely gray. They saw the potential in me that I didn't see in myself. Like Jason Lee's character on *My Name Is Earl*, I have a list (in my mind; actually putting it on paper seemed a bit bizarre) of people I feel I need to make amends with, and more than half are my teachers.

Did you notice that I wrote, "*are* my teachers"? That's because years later, I am still learning from my experiences in their classrooms. I may not have been processing everything at the time, but my ears picked up a lot more than I realized. Today, a week doesn't go by that I don't find myself dissecting a comment, project, or question from one of my teachers through more experienced eyes.

Many college scouts saw my skills on the baseball and football fields, but I couldn't sign their scholarship offers because my grades were too low. Fortunately, another opportunity presented itself in junior college. I was given a second chance to achieve my goal of playing in the NFL. I would have to take a longer route to get there, but it proved to be the right route for me.

Chapter Five

Dean's List

It took a while, but I have chosen to see the hurdles in my life as stepping-stones. Everything happens for a reason, and occasionally it's for a good reason. I didn't do the things I was supposed to do in high school to get to where I wanted to be. I had too much fun, and I had to go to junior college because of my decisions. But while I live with every decision I've made, I don't regret any of them, because I like where I am today. Attending Lackawanna College was a result of bad choices, but it ended up being a turning point in my life.

Lackawanna College is in Scranton, Pennsylvania — a quiet city, famous as the setting of the sitcom *The Office*, that sits comfortably in the Lackawanna River Valley between the Pocono and Endless Mountains. It is a two-year school where many athletes go to receive a second chance; some referred to it as a "Do Over" school. Most of us were there because of our poor grades in high school. Others weren't good enough to get onto a bigger school's team, so they went to Lackawanna to try to better their performance in a short amount of time. Those of us who were there for poor grades had to graduate; those who had gotten good grades in high school could leave after one semester if they found themselves on a bigger school's radar.

Lackawanna recruits all over the country. They get a lot of talent. When I got there, I learned a lot about different people and the places they came from. We had guys on the team from throughout the United States.

There was always a competition about which state produced the best athletes. Of course, I would always say New Jersey, the correct answer. The guys from Florida, California, and Texas would laugh. They thought they were the best at everything in life.

Scranton is a small city, and a lot different from what I was used to. It is very old-fashioned in terms of architecture and vibe. Many buildings resemble medieval castles. The city shuts down at about 9 each night, including weekends. Back in New Jersey and New York, that's when things start to heat up. I had never been to a city that looked like a ghost town once the evening hours hit. We never really had anything to do, because there weren't many places to have fun. There was a tiny mall up the street that had stores none of us wanted to shop at. Also nearby was Scranton University, a very small private school with rich kids who looked down on us. As part of the football team, we were not allowed to go over there — probably because every time we attended one of their parties, a fight would break out and the whole team would be held accountable. Some guys were arrested up there after beating someone up for making racial comments to us.

Scranton gets very cold. The Pocono area is widely known for its harsh winters and its blizzards, which is great for those who choose to live there, but not so much for us football players. The winters were long and dreary. The sun never seemed to come out. It felt as if it snowed every day, even when it wasn't snowing. It was hard getting around when it snowed, and it was hard to get up early in the mornings to make it to class on time. I would wake up in disgust, and my look out the window would confirm what

I expected. We fought every impulse to go back to sleep, and if we had discipline, we made it to class.

Lackawanna only extended a couple of blocks. We had two buildings in which classes were held, and the main building also housed the cafeteria. The food was terrible, but I think that is a required part of the college experience. It was the same thing every day for two years, and it didn't seem all that healthy. Every time we ate in there, guys would say, "Man, we've gotta eat this again? I'm so ready to get out of here."

One of the buildings was a student union with rooms in the back where they put extra tables and chairs to hold classes. We also had a big room with a pool table, a Ping-Pong table, and two televisions. In typical college procrastination style, we spent more time having video-game tournaments than hitting the library.

We had two dormitories, one for the women and one for the men. The men's dorm housed the football, basketball, and baseball teams. Each room had three, sometimes four guys. There was little privacy. We tried to separate our spaces by hanging bed sheets from the ceiling, but we had to be very creative if we wanted to bring our girlfriends back to our rooms; a tie on the door just didn't cut it.

The dorm smelled terrible, because guys would put their football equipment outside their rooms after each practice. The smell of four guys' sweaty clothes wasn't pleasant, either. We had one big bathroom at the end of the hallway on each floor, and that smell lingered as well. Guys would come in from a long night of drinking and vomit all over the bathroom. If it was a Friday night, it would sit there the whole weekend, because the custodians only cleaned during the week. In the basement, we had the washers and dryers, three microwaves that everyone in the dorm used, the locker room, and the weight room. The locker room was old, and the lockers were very small. We could hardly fit anything in them. We had to use these short wooden benches that only fit three guys. The weight room was cramped, too, maybe the size of a large living room. It was like a dungeon, because there were no windows in the basement. It would get very hot and smelly. Guys would have to leave the room between sets to wait for an open machine. Still, we put the work in every day to be great.

Our workouts were very old school. We didn't have the technology or the money for anything fancy. We did abdominal exercises in the basement hallway every day before our regular workout. We would lie down next to each other and get to work. Forty guys lying on the floor in a small hallway was not a pretty sight. If you were late, you could hear the coaches blowing their whistles and counting as they led the workouts. It was tough working out in the basement, but guys who want to work never make excuses. We used what we had to produce results. A hunger develops when you know you have to make do with less. It becomes a driving force on the field when you play opponents who are catered to.

Charles Grande was the weight-room coach, and also the wide-receiver coach. He put extra pressure on his receivers in the weight room. If you didn't work hard there, you would never step on the field. He was a small Italian guy with a very high-pitched voice. It sounded like he was screaming at you all the time.

I did great in my first camp at Lackawanna, but I got myself into the coaches' doghouse early. I made mistake after mistake off the field during the first two weeks. At our very first meeting, I was fooling around with my buddy Javier. Coach Grande was standing in the front of the classroom with his back to us. He was writing plays up on the board, and Javier and I were in the back, acting stupid. Javier said something to me and I laughed, giving him the middle finger. Coach Grande turned around at the same time and caught me in the act. In his high-pitched voice, he yelled, "Get the hell out of my meeting!" When I got outside the door, I heard him say, "I hate freshmen!" I knew he was going to tell the head coach, Mark Duda. I knew the rest of the coaches had heard us, too, because we were right next door to another meeting. Getting on the coaches' wrong side was the last thing I wanted to do, as they held the key to my future. But I hadn't really changed from high school.

The next mistake I made was partying when I wasn't supposed to. We had been going through practice for some days and finally had a day off, but we still had a curfew. We decided to go to a club in the middle of the night anyway. There were security guards at the campus entrance, so we couldn't just walk out the front door, but Javier had a gate coming from his window that we could use to climb down to the ground. We got back from the club around 2 a.m. and were climbing back through the window. I was the last person to go. As I watched one of my teammates climb, I saw flashlights coming around the side of the building. Two security guards were doing a routine check. I didn't say a word to my friend, who was halfway up the gate. I just took off running. I heard the guards yell for me to stop, but I never looked back or slowed down. I ran three blocks up the street and sat down in an alley. I knew they would find out my name and I would be in trouble again. I had gotten in trouble with Javier multiple times, but I just knew Coach Duda would send me home this time. Surprisingly, he didn't, but I was in deep.

I always waited for my teammates to come up with a catchy nickname for me, like Lefty, since I couldn't get right. But somehow, even though I did everything to stop myself from being successful during my younger years, I kept getting chances.

To this day, I remain friends with many of my teammates from Lackawanna. They became my family away from family. We had our tough times, as every family does, but we worked it out. My time there didn't start out that way, though. My first training camp was rough. The sophomores on the team tried to take shots at me any chance they got. I was a freshman with the potential to get some playing time, so they were trying to see if I could handle everything.

In junior college, guys might be a little older than your normal student. Half of the team was above typical college age. We had guys who were 27 years old. These were grown men I was playing against at 18, and they were good. Our defense was big, mean, and fast. They didn't care who you were. They were going to let you know when they hit you. Every time I caught a pass, there were multiple guys coming at me. If they couldn't get to me in time, they would scream in my ear to make sure I knew they would get a good shot on me at some point. The coaches embraced that type of play. They wanted to see if we could handle it psychologically as well as physically.

There was one time I almost got into a fight in the locker room with a teammate. He threw my equipment on the floor in a joking manner, but I didn't find it funny. I lunged to fight him. I didn't know these guys, and coming from Plainfield, I was still hanging on to the inner-city mentality. The other sophomores immediately stepped between us, saying, "All our issues are settled on the field." So we did the smart thing and didn't fight each other. Instead, we took care of it on the field. That type of leadership was crucial.

It was very hot that first summer, and the coaches would wake us up with whistles every morning. It was really tough in the beginning. I remember thinking to myself, "Am I cut out for this?" I loved football, but this was a big adjustment for me. I was used to being spoiled because I was the man, or I thought I was. When I got to Lackawanna, I was just your average guy, which led to a mini-identity crisis. It was the first time in my life that I had felt ordinary.

I hated the coaches my first few weeks at Lackawanna. I thought they were crazy. Growing up, all my coaches were cool. I knew them from the town. They watched me grow up. They knew my parents. They showed me respect. They were more of the players' type of coaches. They joked with us all the time. They understood us. The coaches at Lackawanna couldn't care less about my feelings and ego.

Our trainer was old school and very hard on us. If you had an injury, most of the time it was just, "Ice it!" She didn't play around. You quickly learned not to go into her room unless you had broken something. She would tape ankles every day without pre-wrap. As we walked in she would scream, "Go shave your legs before you come over here to get taped." I think they wanted us to face these conditions every day so that we would strive for better ones in the future.

Our practices were at a minor-league baseball field. At the time, it was the home of the Philadelphia Phillies' minor-league team. It now belongs to the Scranton/Wilkes-Barre Yankees. The stadium was a ways from the school, so we had to get on yellow buses every morning. It had the old AstroTurf, which rips your skin off as soon as you land on it. I didn't have any turf shoes, so I wore New Balance sneakers that were not made for football. They had no ankle support, but they got the job done for me.

We had a few practice facilities at Lackawanna, because our normal field would turn to mud by the fourth week of the season. In Scranton, the weather was always bad in the fall, which made it much harder to get quality work done in practice. (Note: If your moods are tied to the weather, as mine are, make sure you research the climate of the college you select.) The weather did, though, have the side effect of equipping us to handle any type of conditions we might play in.

We had a field two blocks from campus that we called the Pumpkin Patch. It was made of a mixture of grass and asphalt and looked like something formed a million years ago. We didn't have our own game field. We had to play at a local high school's field, a 15-minute ride from campus. We would get drunk after our games on Saturday nights and walk over to the Pumpkin Patch. We made a pact that we would get plastered after every game we won, and the party gods must have been on our side, because we won every game my first season. We would get drunk with nothing to do and nowhere to go. We would just sit in the hallways or in our rooms until we passed out. We never considered the effect it was having on our bodies. Then, on Sunday mornings, we would go to the Pumpkin Patch to get our bodies loose after the Saturday battles.

Our time at Lackawanna consisted of a lot of reminiscing on what we could have done. We would sit in our dorm rooms and talk about the universities that had recruited us out of high school. We would compare how many scholarship offers we each had. We would critique one another's highlight films until the wee hours. A few of my teammates were from the nation's capital, so of course I would say, "I'd smash ya boys in DC." We would talk about how different things would have been if we had just paid attention in high school. We would sit on a stoop in front of our dorm and talk about how boring it was in Scranton, Pennsylvania. There was one gas station in the area that we could walk to, directly across the street from the dorm. We would go get snacks, come back, and sit on the stoop and stare at nothing. "I can't wait to get out of here," each of us would say. "I'm never coming back." We were disappointed in ourselves for being there. We couldn't wait to be able to showcase our talent on the national level like the guys we watched on television, whom most of us had played with or against in high school. We all felt we were good enough to be on that level, and a few of us were.

I speak as if everything was bad at Lackawanna, but the truth is, I needed that culture shock. Coach Duda ran a solid program. His coaching style either whipped you into the right mindset or sent you packing. He never bluffed when he said, "I'll send your ass home." He had to make sure we understood that he was the captain and that he wasn't going to let any of us mess up his ship. He tried to run his program as if it were Division I, so that we knew what to expect when we left. He gave us enough rope to hang ourselves with, but he was still on us to do better. He was everything I needed coming out of high school. He was the person who really changed my way of thinking and, in turn, changed my life.

I was slated to be a starter at wide receiver, but I sat on the bench for our first game. I hated it; I had never done that to the point where I didn't set foot on the field for an entire game. Coach Duda was serious this time. My instincts were pushing me to go up to him after the game and demand to know why he'd had me suit up if I wasn't going to play, but that was when the light bulb finally illuminated. In a moment of clarity that lasted less than a minute but is forever etched in my brain, I went from being irate with my coach, to being embarrassed because I had been talking it up before the game, to my epiphany. It wasn't that I had let myself down again, but something far worse: I had let the team down, and my ridiculousness off the field could have cost us a win. From that point on, it was like someone had handed me super-strength prescription glasses. Everything was suddenly in focus. The next game, I was back in my starting spot, and I never looked back. I wanted to be a key contributor to the team. I was too good to sit on the bench for stupid mistakes I was making off the field.

I had to learn college ball quickly. It moved a lot faster than high-school ball, and I couldn't do some of my trademark moves. I also had to learn defenses. Our coaches in high school hadn't taught us anything about coverages or how to read them. In college, coverages would change in the middle of a play, and that was not what I was used to. I also had to adjust to the way we ran practices. Everything was scripted and organized. In high school, we had no script; we just did what we did. We never paid attention in practice unless something affected us directly. But Coach Duda and Coach Grande didn't allow any playing around or talking in the back. We had to keep busy and be tuned in. I was behind everyone in football IQ, but I made it my business to get caught up quickly. My teammates taught me a lot on the run. We genuinely looked out for one another. They knew I was crucial to the success of the team, and they made sure I knew what I had to know to do my part.

I had to get used to being a student-athlete once the school year started. We had study halls every morning at 7. It was the coaches' way of making sure we were up for 8 a.m. classes. We would sit in study hall and do homework or prepare for any test we had that day. We would be dead tired, having stayed up very late because we weren't used to living without strict parents. A coach always sat with us to make sure we did something in study hall. Sometimes Coach Duda's wife would sit in. She played hardball with us: "Don't think because I am in here that you guys can get over. I'll send your asses home myself." Coach had no tolerance for guys missing study hall. There were no excuses or exceptions. If you missed a certain number, he kicked you off the team. He didn't care who you were. There were players who missed too many times, and they just disappeared.

It may not sound like a big deal, but one of my proudest moments of that school year was my perfect attendance at study hall, because I was trying to embrace the concept of "loving the process as much as the product." All the pieces, electrifying and dull, fit together.

But in the middle of my first semester, I nearly made one mistake that could have changed my life forever. One of my teammates sold drugs to people throughout the school. He was a freshman who had arrived at Lackawanna with me, so we had become cool. One of my other teammates had done some transactions with him. They tried to pull me in, saying, "Ay, what's good, you want in? It's easy in here. We only sell to the guys in the dorms and the white boys in the school. They're spending a lot of money just for weed. That's all we're selling, nothing hard. All you have to do is take a ride with me to Philadelphia and bring some back." At first, I wanted no part. Then I decided that I might take a shot at it, because I had no extra cash, and relying on the cafeteria three times a day was breaking me down. I could have easily called back home for some money, but once again, I was about to make the wrong choice.

I thought about it overnight. The next day, there were police dressed in black searching the dorms. I then found out that the guy who was selling the drugs had killed a few people in Philadelphia and was on the run. He had come to Lackawanna to try to hide. When the police raided the dorms, they found multiple guns in his room that had been linked to crimes. I could easily have gone on that ride with him and been taken down for something I had no idea about. And that wouldn't be the last time I teetered on making a decision that could have changed my life forever.

In fact, I was almost kicked out of school during my first semester for a huge academic mistake. One of my teammates was in my computer class. We were cramming for a project. I finished mine, and he came to me and asked if he could use my paper as a guide for his. Everyone knows you can be kicked out of school for plagiarism, but of course I let him check out my paper. Yet he didn't change any of the words around on his — all he did was change the name, as if we were back in middle school. A few days later, the teacher approached us after class. "I can have you both kicked out of school for this," she said, but instead, "I am going to give you guys 100 on the paper, to split between the both of you. This means you will both get a

50. If I see this again, I am going to report you both to the school and your coach."

As you can see, I wasn't ready for college, and I had to learn, repeatedly, the hard way. Any of the mistakes I made early in my freshman year could have ended my college career. And with all this craziness happening within the first few months, I was weary about what the rest of the school year had in store for me.

During the spring semester, we had 5 a.m. workouts. Some players had to be there before 5 because of something they had done. If you were late for one workout, Coach Duda kicked you off the team. From there, we went straight to study hall. From study hall, we went straight to class. We had our normal classes, and then practice at 3 p.m. I took night classes after practice during the spring, too. I hated spring semesters. The days dragged along. It didn't warm up until the end of April, sometimes May. It was very depressing. That was the life of a student-athlete in Scranton. Coach made it just how it would be at the next level.

The atmosphere at Lackawanna made our team a family. Only 50 to 100 people showed up for our games, so we played for one another. Most guys were from states far away, and their families couldn't make it to more than one game a year. I should have been playing in front of 50,000 fans weekly. Instead, you could hear a pin drop at our games. But because of that, we did everything as a team. We went out to eat as a team. We partied as a team. We got in trouble as a team. That mentality made us good on the field. Nobody could beat us, because we were all we had. We all trusted one another, on and off the field. Our defense didn't give up more than seven touchdowns that entire undefeated season. That was crucial, because we were young on the offensive side and still had growing pains to go through. The defense carried us.

One week, we traveled to Buffalo to play Erie Community College. They changed their homecoming week to face us in the middle of the season. We had a great game, but I was also focused on something else: Their stadium was directly across the street from the Bills' stadium. When we pulled up for an away game, I would always do a walkthrough of the field, just to get a feel for what it was like. Here, I came out onto the field with my phone in my hand. I stood at the gate and looked across the street in amazement. I thought to myself, *maybe one day I could play in a stadium like that.* At the time, I didn't think it would actually happen. I had a dream of playing in front of 80,000, but it was such a long shot. I called my dad to share how incredible it was to see this stadium. "Dad, we're out here in Buffalo, New York, playing right across from the Bills' stadium," I said. "I'm telling you, one day I'm going to be playing in a stadium like that." He replied, "You go get what's yours. If you want to play in that stadium, don't let anything stop you. Only you can stop yourself."

My first year at Lackawanna was mentally draining. The team was good, we were winning every week, and I was a starter; that should have been enough for me, but it wasn't. I didn't get passes thrown to me like I thought I should. As a wide receiver, I wanted the ball, but our offense was running-based. We rarely threw the ball. When we did, I was never the first target. The play would have to break down in order for me to get a pass. I was used to this, having gone through the same thing in high school until my senior year. Still, I would complain to my family: "Ma, I'm not getting any passes. This is terrible, because I'm always open." My family would reply, "Say something to the quarterback. He's the one on the field throwing the ball. Tell his ass that if he doesn't throw you the ball, he is going to have to deal with me." That at least put a smile on my face. I wasn't actually going to say something like that — as part of the team, I never wanted to disrupt things or jeopardize any future opportunities to get the ball. The only thing I could do was to handle what I could handle and continue to work hard. Even though it hurt, I knew that my time would soon come.

Our team ended up in the top 10 of the National Junior College Athletic Association. We played a bowl game out in Glendale, Arizona. Glendale Community College was a powerhouse every year, and that trip was a lot of fun. We stayed out there for a week and practiced at their school. Their team would come out to watch us and talk junk. One guy came up, started talking some smack, and spat on our bus. The night before the game, we had a dinner banquet with them, and there was almost a fight in the bathroom. We felt they were disrespecting us. Once again, we were about to get in trouble as a team. We didn't care. We had no respect for them, and it was on from there. We beat up on them in that game. It came down to the last drive: We drove the distance of the field and scored in under a minute. We beat them and celebrated in their hometown that night.

Most of my teammates that year went on to play at D1-A schools. Several went on to have stints in the NFL. That was the most talented team I ever played on. It was also the biggest family I had been a part of. That was what made us so good. We were like a military platoon: a collection of guys willing to put their lives on the line for one another.

I also turned my grades around. I was on the dean's list almost every semester. Going into my sophomore season, I didn't want any recruiters to say to our coaches that I still lacked the grades to make it into their school. Focusing on my schoolwork also helped me focus on the field. It taught me what hard work could get me.

That sophomore season was my season. I decided to stay on campus for the summer session so I could work out with the team. A lot of our players did the same, so we were able to get good work in. Everyone wanted to win. Everyone wanted to go on and play D1-A. I was voted team captain, just like in my senior year of high school there was no excuse for not being there.

My teammates always looked up to me. I was never a person who spoke a lot, but I always led by example. I worked harder than anyone else — first one on the field and last one off. I wanted to play D1-A, and I wasn't going to let anything stop me. I worked out twice a day. I did extra ab work in my room. On the weekends, I went up to the weight room. Sometimes teammates would go up there with me, other times I would go by myself, but there was never a weekend I didn't go. Some guys went home every weekend. I hardly ever went home, because I felt as if I was finally on the right track, and this train was not making any unnecessary stops or pickups.

Some of my teammates were with me very consistently. Every weekend, we would work out and talk about what we would do if we made it to the NFL. We would say things like, "When I make it to the big leagues, I'm getting two cars. I want a nice house and my parents to have a house. I can't wait to get out of here so that I can really showcase my talent. I know I could make it up there." We always had the NFL Network on during our workouts to motivate us. I dreamed big. I was determined to get there, but I had a lot of work to do. I was determined that nobody would outwork me

— not on our team and not in the country. I felt like a failure if I missed even one workout. Everything I did was football-related. Everything I watched was football-related. I became the ultimate student of the game, going for his Ph.D. I knew I could play at that level. I just needed a chance to prove it.

My sophomore season turned out to be a good one personally, and I scored a decent number of touchdowns. Unfortunately, the team didn't do as well as we had hoped. We lost three games, and there was no excuse for that. Anything short of what we had done the year before was unacceptable. We had the talent to go undefeated again, but we didn't come together as a family that second season. It seemed everyone was playing primarily for his own stats. My teammates were more worried about getting to the next level than winning games at this level. They were playing more for the name on the back of the uniform than the name on the front.

Our last game of the season was away against Georgia Military. It was way down in the country. We went by bus, and it took a long time to get there, because we made a few stops on the way to let guys stretch and eat. I knew I had to perform well, because there would be a lot of recruiters in the crowd.

We came out for warm-ups, special teams first. The special teams are usually the skilled position players, or the smaller players. The next group to come out is usually the middle-size players, the linebackers and tight ends. Since Georgia Military was the home team, the last group to come out was their linemen. They were the biggest group of players I had ever seen on one team. I was instantly anxious, because I had never been hit by someone that big. I didn't want to get hit by one of those dudes.

They also had players who had committed to big schools already. The whole week leading up to the game, we studied one of their safeties, who had committed to the University of Illinois. He was a big guy and a big hitter. "Hey, D. Jones, you better not get hit by this boy," my teammates teased. "Man, please. He has to catch me first," I replied, trying to act as if I wasn't the least bit nervous. I thrived on playing against the best talent, because it was the perfect gauge for where my skills were at. I loved competition. If I could perform well against the very best, I knew I would get offers.

I had a great game. I made many big plays, including a touchdown. After the game, a few Division I coaches came up to me and told me they would be in touch. Most of them stayed true to their word. At the time, I really wanted to go to the University of Mississippi, and they made it clear they wanted me. I was excited because they were in the Southeastern Conference, which is the most respected in the country. It's like a farm system for the NFL. Every other school I talked to told me they liked me but questioned my speed.

I decided to commit to Ole Miss. I was ecstatic. I let everyone back home know that my hard work had finally paid off. My parents were especially happy, because I would finally get what I wanted and we wouldn't have to pay tuition anymore.

A few weeks later, I went home for Thanksgiving. I was eager to let everyone know the news. I attended my high school's traditional Thanksgiving football game, and everyone already knew where I was going and congratulated me. But then I went home to watch football on television. The line across the bottom of the screen read that the coaching staff at Ole

Miss had been fired. I was in shock. I had no clue what was going on or what to do. I called Coach Duda to see what he thought, and he had no idea what to do either. He just said, "Wait and see what happens. You should be okay. We know how good you are. Hopefully they see it too and keep you."

But the new coaching staff came in, and they didn't like me. They said they didn't want any junior college guys unless they were coming in January. I didn't believe that. When I called them, they had no explanation but made sure to mention that they wouldn't be honoring my scholarship, because it had only been a verbal deal. I was hurt. I was lost. I couldn't understand why this was happening to me. I thought I had done everything right this time.

So, here we went again. It was back to the grind. I began sending my film to coaches around the country. I called coaches myself, just as I had in high school. It was my life, and I couldn't leave it up to anyone else to help me get recruited. But the phone in my hand became an instrument of searing pain as each coach I called said things like, "We like the way you play, but we don't think you're fast enough." Others said, "We love your talent, but we don't have the scholarships. Would you be willing to walk on?" Some were more blunt: "We don't think you're ready for this level." All of my teammates had already committed. I was the only one without a place to go. I had so many regrets at that time: I knew if I had just done my work in high school, I wouldn't have been in this position.

There wasn't much time left until National Signing Day, and all I could think was, "Why me?" I was doing everything right. I had turned my life around. I was focused. I just wanted to pursue my dreams. Why didn't anybody want me when my coaches were telling me how good I was? I thought maybe they were only telling me I was good because they had to.

But while it hurt that nobody wanted me, my whole life I'd had to fight for what I wanted, so I stayed strong. I knew it wasn't going to be easy. I could easily have thrown in the towel at that point and said I was done playing. But I had a goal I was still working toward, and nothing was going to stop me.

I decided I would go to any college with a football team, even one with as terrible weather as Lackawanna. If I were good enough, the NFL would find me.

Youngstown State University contacted me at the last minute. The coach who recruited me was a great salesman. He informed me of their upcoming schedule, which included an away game at Ohio State University. "Imagine having a great game in front of 100,000 people," he said with a smile. "We need some wide receivers. You'll probably come in and start from day one. I've seen your video, and you are better than what we have." He made me feel like he really wanted me. He also used the line I most wanted to hear, that I would be an automatic starter coming in. He sold me when he said the team played major D1-A schools every year. I knew that if I had strong games against them, it would look good on my résumé for the NFL.

YSU is a small school, but I had heard a lot about them because I was doing my homework. I knew they had a strong history of winning seasons. There was a catch, though: Yet again, I wouldn't be on a full scholarship. I would have to earn it, just as I had my second year at Lackawanna. But I was out of options at that point.

I signed my letter of intent to YSU on National Signing Day with the rest of my teammates, who inked their deals with bravado because they would be on full scholarships. Nonetheless, I was excited to be able to move on to the next level and represent Lackawanna College. My family was ecstatic as well. Unfortunately, I couldn't say the same for the 60 or so players who had come in with my freshman class. Only eight of us made it to graduation. It was sad to see so many guys fail out of school because they couldn't get their acts together. I couldn't worry about them, though, because I had my own work to do. Plus, I was about to be blindsided by some health issues.

One day during my last semester at Lackawanna, we were playing basketball, as we often did just to stay in shape. I began to feel nauseated, like I was suddenly coming down with a virus. I went to the bathroom and almost passed out from what I saw. My urine was all blood and bubbles. The craziest thoughts began running through my head. I went to the hospital, and they told me something was wrong with my kidneys. I was bewildered, because I was more in shape than I had ever been from the rigors of college football. Plus, before this little episode, I had felt great. I hadn't shown signs of any sickness before. "These doctors don't know what they are talking about," I said to myself. That is what any 19- or 20-year-old would say.

The doctors at the hospital recommended that I see a nephrologist — a kidney specialist — so I went to one in New Jersey. The biopsy procedure he did was painful: I had to lie on my stomach as he inserted a very long instrument into my back. The instrument looked like a long needle with a big handle on the end where the doctor held it. It had a button he pushed to clamp off a piece of my kidney. It made a loud sound, and I could feel it squeezing inside of me. The doctor did it two more times because he needed multiple pieces. I had to be awake for the whole procedure; he needed me to hold my breath when he stuck the needle into my back because when you breathe, your kidneys move up and down. Afterward, I had to lie flat on my back for five or six hours to prevent internal bleeding. I couldn't work out for another week after that because the doctor didn't want me to take any unnecessary risks.

The biopsy revealed that I had IgA nephropathy, in which an antibody called IgA builds up in the kidneys, causing inflammation and, eventually, loss of kidney function. You know you have something bad when you can't even pronounce it. The doctors told me that it was rare in African-Americans. I was the only person in my family with kidney disease, so it couldn't be hereditary. I slipped right into the first stage of grief, which is denial, and that was the worst thing I could possibly have done.

After the diagnosis, the doctors wanted to put me on steroids, along with fish-oil pills. I decided I didn't want to do that, because it would weaken my playing ability. I wasn't sure of this, but everything I had heard or read said that steroids had many side effects, and that that was one of them. Plus, they said that the pills gave off a fishy smell, and being in college and having the most fun of my life, I didn't want to walk around with stank breath. But most of all, I didn't want to take pills every day. I was stuck in denial. The doctors couldn't be right. Maybe if I sent them highlight videos like I had to college coaches, they would see that I was in my prime. I couldn't imagine the disease affecting me the way it did. So I went on without the steroids, living as if I had never been diagnosed with anything. That was a mistake.

I ended up graduating from Lackawanna with an associate's degree in communications. Walking across that stage was one of my biggest achievements to that point. I had finally done something positive academically. Hard work had finally paid off in one aspect of my life. I had come so far from my days at Plainfield High School. I had come a long way from climbing out of classroom windows to leave with my boys. I was one of the first in my family to finish any higher level of education. I had made my family proud for something other than sports.

But I couldn't stop there. My mission wasn't complete. I wanted to prove wrong everyone who had passed on me. I wanted to prove to myself that I could do it. And I wanted to prove to everyone back home that they could make it out, no matter what their circumstances were.

My time at Lackawanna College was exactly what I needed to get my life on track. When I entered the school, I was just another trouble-making freshman who thought he knew it all. I didn't appreciate the grit and dedication needed to be a college athlete. I had a dream of playing in the NFL, but no recipe. The sad thing is that it really wasn't hard for me to do well in school. I just had to come to terms with the fact that I needed to be the best at everything I did, on and off the field, if I wanted to achieve my goal. Schoolwork wasn't an option; it was a must.

I became the team captain because I worked hard in all areas of my life. I became one of the best players to come through the school because I wanted it. It all happened with focus and dedication. During my years at

Lackawanna, I changed those dreams into attainable goals. Coach Duda brought a different mentality out of me. He gave me that second chance.

Chapter Six

The NFL Works Closely with the FBI

Youngstown State University was the next step along my bumpy brick road. I started with a partial scholarship; I was forced to earn a full one, which was an added pressure.

YSU's campus is small but welcoming. On my first day walking around campus, I was moved by the contrast between the traditional brick-and-mortar buildings, which whispered to students that a solid education needed to be assembled with precision, one piece at a time, and the state-of-the-art buildings, which declared that while becoming more educated was the goal, developing your style was what would make you stand out in life.

Surprisingly, I didn't experience an awkward adjustment period when I moved to Youngstown. I had this feeling from the start that I was meant to be there, and I had an overwhelming sense of belonging even before taking my first class — compared with Lackawanna, where I always felt away from home. My friends who attended Rutgers University in New Brunswick, New Jersey, claimed they preferred an atmosphere where they met new people every day, which was certainly beneficial for them, because they weren't exactly earning the best reputations. On the other hand, with their classes spread out over five campuses, they experienced daily frustrations with late or packed buses, which caused them to arrive to many classes tardy or not at all.

Youngstown, Ohio, which is an hour's drive southeast of Cleveland and northwest of Pittsburgh, has been dealing with depression, oppression, and poverty for decades. The people of Youngstown are starving for something big to happen for their city. When a few new friends and I explored the off-campus surroundings, I was the only one who didn't seem put off by the ever-present drug dealers and homeless people on the street corners, because they were an expected part of the scenery in New Jersey. The biggest difference between Youngstown and back home was that while in New Jersey, we had our fair share of poverty-stricken areas, in Youngstown, house after house had been foreclosed on. I couldn't imagine where people lived, because there didn't seem to be many houses to live in.

I never really wanted to leave campus. I never wanted to be caught in the wrong neighborhood and have something bad happen to me just because I wasn't from around there.

Even though I wasn't from Youngstown, I felt a connection to the city from day one and took it upon myself to give it some hope. I felt I could relate to what these people were going through. I became one of the Youngstown boys. I wanted to show them that, with the right instruments added to their toolbox, they could make it out of there.

During my first summer there, the coaches arranged for me to stay with a few of my teammates. Five of us lived in a house that was very big and old, as were many of the houses on that street. At first, I feared that with five guys from the football team living together, we would all want to throw a party every night, but it was much worse than that: My housemates were incredibly boring. They played video games from sunup to sundown. There were days when I could have sworn they only left that living room for the bathroom, and it wasn't to use the shower. I decided that I would just leave the house and go to the stadium to work out by myself, because the bad habits of others have a way of latching onto you. I would go meet with the coaches to learn the playbook. I had to do something to occupy my time, and I figured it should be productive. I figured it should be something that would help me get better and earn a starting spot faster. I didn't have time to play around all day. I only had a couple of weeks to secure a starting spot. I had to earn my scholarship.

But when I got back from the stadium every day, I had other concerns to deal with, foremost being that my housemates never cleaned up. They would leave dishes in the sink for days or weeks at a time. I didn't understand how they could do that and then have the audacity to invite women over. My second gripe was that the fridge was regularly empty, because we didn't have any money. We couldn't work at serious jobs because of NCAA regulations. We could only earn a certain amount of money per week. There were times when we didn't have hot water because we couldn't pay the bills. I took showers at the stadium because the water at home was so cold. I didn't even have a real bed. All I had was an air mattress, which I had brought from back home. The only things in my room were the air mattress, my television, and a radio to listen to my own music. I brought my bike from home so that I could get around without driving everywhere. A full tank of gas was a rare luxury. Something had to give.

Most people believe that the sports stars they see on television are very well off. Let's go one step further: If we took a poll, I think it is safe to say that an overwhelming majority of the public would argue that these athletes make too much money. That brings us to Shabazz Napier. (No, this isn't another one of my quizzes. But now that I think about it, I will be adding it to my repertoire the next time I speak at a school, just to see what sort of feedback I get.) Shabazz Napier earned the MVP title at the 2014 NCAA Men's Basketball Championship for his incredible performance for the University of Connecticut during March Madness. In an interview, shortly after winning the title for his school, Napier stunned every journalist in the room, all of whom were probably anticipating an "I'm going to Disney World" moment. So, what was the shot heard around the basketball world that he served up? "There are hungry nights that I go to bed and I am starving."

That's right: The number one player at one of the top basketball colleges in the country, who earns millions of dollars for his school, goes to bed hungry. In a tournament where Warren Buffett offered $1 billion to the person who could fill out a perfect bracket, the star player is struggling to make ends meet. Seeing as nobody won that bracket challenge, and Warren Buffett got all that free publicity, I think the gentleman's thing for Mr. Buffett to do would be to donate just a tiny percentage of that prize money, let's say 1 percent, to an NCAA student-athlete scholarship. Trust me, he wouldn't lose any sleep over giving away $10 million, and if he did make that donation, a lot of struggling student-athletes wouldn't lose another night of sleep, either.

Before summer workout sessions began, my coaches set me up with a job so that I could have some type of income and keep busy. I would have gone crazy sitting in the house, watching my teammates play video games all day. Under NCAA regulations, we could only work a certain number of hours while on scholarship, and only in the summertime. I worked in a fireworks factory. The warehouse was blazing hot every day, and I didn't get along with the bosses too well. I didn't like the way they spoke to us, but I needed the job, so I stayed quiet.

Once our team sessions started, I would go to work in the morning and then to workouts in the afternoon. If I wasn't at the factory, I was at the stadium getting better. There was little leisure time, but it didn't feel like work, because I enjoyed the grueling routine. Some of the players went to workouts in the morning and then to work in the afternoon, mostly so they wouldn't have to run in the heat. But I felt running at the hottest hours would get me ready for training camp. I enjoyed the feeling after a great workout in the heat. Every day I was becoming a better person, and after a workout I would feel like a better person than I had been the day before. That is the greatest path to be on: one toward self-actualization. Even though there is no end, because there will always be some area you can strengthen, striving to do better and be better every day means finding yourself on the ultimate path of enlightenment, and that leads to pure satisfaction.

One summer afternoon, we had a seven-on-seven practice. Only skilled position players compete in those, so the linemen just watched. There weren't any coaches, because they couldn't come out to watch yet under NCAA rules (which made no sense, because the players on the sidelines used their phones to record most plays). That was the first time I met most of the team. It was also my first time playing in our stadium, known as the Ice Castle. We began to run plays, and I felt as if all eyes were on me. The linemen had the most fun, because they weren't suited up and could run commentary on how the new guys did. I wanted to show them that I was there and that I meant business. I couldn't have cared less about making friends. The reality was that my goal was to come in and take someone's spot.

Right from the first set of play, I felt I was better than most of the guys on the field. I also felt more competitive than any of them. It was obvious that my road to get there had been bumpier than theirs. There was another wide receiver on the team who got the ball thrown to him on almost all of the non-run plays. I try never to hate on anybody, but I was clearly better than him. I wasn't being cocky. I was being confident. (I've always differentiated between the two in that confidence stays on the inside, while being cocky is letting it out.) If I felt that someone else thought differently about my abilities, I did what I could to change that. He was their guy at the time, so I had to earn their respect. As a natural competitor, I have a simple formula for anything important in life: Find the best at what you want to do, and then become better than the best.

One day, we took a trip out to the University of Akron for a scrimmage. I was excited: Since they were D1-A, and supposedly better than us, this was an opportunity to prove to my teammates how good I really was. I had a field day against Akron. I caught passes left and right. I caught passes I shouldn't have caught, and I took them all the way to the end zone a couple of times. I took offense to the notion of their being better than us. I made it personal, as I always did. The guys from Akron took notice, as did my teammates. They asked me why I was at YSU and not a bigger school. I overheard my own teammates whispering about how good I was. I was on a mission. I had the heaviest chip on my shoulder. They were my teammates, and we were buddies, but I had goals. I couldn't achieve my goals by worrying about their feelings. I had to take what was mine. Now it was time for my coaches to realize it.

It was hot and hazy almost every day when we started training camp. I was having a great time. I caught passes over people as if I were in a Madden video game. I wanted the coaches to see that I was a valuable asset to the team. Outwardly, I was humble about it, but I still felt I was the best at my position. The coaches had told me they were considering redshirting me, which would mean I wouldn't play in a single game that season. I couldn't let that happen. I already felt disrespected by the partial scholarship. I used these insults as fuel and, just like that, I became a starter.

Once the season began, though, I noticed a pattern that I had gotten very used to. Our quarterback almost never threw me the ball, and it became apparent whom the coaches favored. It was as if they hadn't seen me play at all during the summer. I didn't understand what was going on. I wanted to scream at everybody, from the coaches to the quarterback. I felt like he had all the power. He had to be seeing me wide open on the field. (Most great wide receivers are convinced that they are always open, but I really was. And I still have the videotapes to prove it.) The coaches didn't even call plays that were designed for me to get the ball. Once again, the play would have to break down in order for me to get a chance. Everybody else could see it. We would go back and look at film, and I would constantly be wide open. The other guys would ask me why the quarterback was not throwing me the ball. I suspected the coaches had told him not to.

To add to the humiliation, we were losing most of our matches. Game after game, it was the same thing: I hardly got any passes, and we lost. It was nothing like Lackawanna. At least at Lackawanna, we won. I told my family over and over that I hated being there. I wanted to leave. The city was depressing, the coaches ignored me, and we kept losing.

We only won four games my first year at YSU. It was the first time I had ever been on a losing team. The feeling was foreign to me, but somehow, it didn't really bother my teammates. I couldn't understand it. This never would have happened back at Lackawanna. This team wasn't a family. This team wasn't mean enough. We had too many players who only cared about themselves and how they could raise their stats. We had way too many cliques, and too many guys who didn't want to work hard. During meetings, my teammates messed around all the time. Those who didn't play much sat in the back and fooled around. (Yes, it was like watching a younger version of myself.) They didn't want to go the extra mile in the weight room, and they wouldn't get in the faces of people who cut their workouts short. They just wanted to be on the team so that they could go to school for free. We couldn't win like that. For any team to win, there has to be one goal. We had 80 different goals in that locker room.

After my first season at YSU, I decided to transfer. I was even willing to go down to Division 2 just to be out of there, because I knew that if I transferred to a school in the same division or up one, I would lose a year of eligibility. I began calling coaches around the country. I called my friend Rasoul, who was attending Hampton University. I asked him to talk to his coaches so that I could transfer there. I called all of my former teammates from Lackawanna to see if they would talk to their coaches. But none of the schools wanted me. I didn't understand it. I knew I was good. I wanted to play against them just to make them pay for overlooking me.

Things were not working out for my transferring. Nothing was working out for me.

I always kept my family in the loop. They didn't like my quarterback or my coaches. "Stop being so nice," my father and uncles would tell me. "Tell them to start throwing you the ball. You are not out there for your health, running routes and putting in work. You are trying to get to the next level. If you don't say something, we will!" I didn't care anymore; I just wanted to leave. But they told me to stick it out. "It will get better," they assured me. They never wanted to let me quit anything. My father told me I was tougher than that, and I was good enough to make the coaches notice me. He told me if I just kept working hard, I would be okay. So I decided to stay.

Things would eventually get better — but not before I almost threw it all away.

I had been on the straight and narrow ever since my early days at Lackawanna, when I learned how fast one could get derailed. But when the season started, I moved out of my original house and into another house with three friends. Drugs and drug exchanges moved through our apartment. These drugs were being transported in through various channels.

My grandmother always told me, "You will deal with the consequences for the decisions you make." Well, I decided to live in that house for the whole semester. I knew what my housemates were doing, but I didn't know the logistics of it. I purposely stayed away from all of their illegal interactions, just in case the police ever found out. I went to class every day, then to practice, then home. I never got in a car with them or went anywhere that looked suspicious. I never wanted to give anyone a reason to associate me with their shenanigans.

One day, I overheard one of them say, "Hey, that package from California didn't come in the mail this week. That's the first time it's happened; do you think something's wrong?" He was afraid that the cops had intercepted the package and found what was inside. He became extremely paranoid and began moving everything incriminating out of our house.

One night, I came home to a party that one of my housemates had thrown together. There was a mixture of people I knew and people I didn't. The season was over, so we were celebrating the opportunity to relax. There was a guy at the party I had never seen before. They told me he was a friend of one of my housemates and had come in from California. I figured he had come to bring a package, but I never knew the details. I never even got his real name. He looked very suspicious, like one of those shady guys in the movies, but I didn't pay it much attention. I went on partying and celebrating with the people I knew.

The next morning, things really started to feel strange. It was right before Thanksgiving break, and since I was heading home for the long weekend, my stuff was packed. I woke up to a phone call from one of my friends. "Hey, the police stopped my girl's car this morning and searched it for no reason," he said. *No reason! Was he kidding me? Right, you guys are the warm and friendly drug dealers.* Then it hit me: The two of us had been in her car the night before. It was weird for them to search her. She wasn't the type to get into any trouble. She had great grades and was on track to graduate. They had no reason to search her car. That was the first sign that something was about to happen. My roommates came back for a while, and then walked out of the house an hour later. They were going down to the probation office, as one of them had messed up in the past. I was in the kitchen cooking breakfast as they walked out.

Three minutes later, my phone rang. My roommate screamed, "SWAT team is outside!" His voice was trembling, so I knew it was no joke. Before I could say anything, there was a banging on the door. "Open up, it's the police!" I was terrified. "Open the damn door!" Everything shifted to slow motion. I opened the door, expecting to see some smug cops' mugs, but within a few inches of my face were the recently polished barrels of their guns. They stood there with their guns drawn on me. I didn't want to make any sudden moves or give them any reason to think I was going to do something crazy, and have someone with a happy trigger finger end me.

"What's your name, son?"

My life flashed before my eyes. I couldn't get this far and end up in jail now for something I had nothing to do with. I was doing everything the right way. I had only decided to stay in that house because I was too lazy to move my things in the middle of the semester. I had known that one day my roommates' game would unravel; I had just prayed it would be after I left. I had planned on moving after the semester ended. Why hadn't I just left once I knew they were doing something wrong? That decision could have changed my life forever, and I had done nothing. I could have been sucked into the whole mess if one of the officers had doubted anything I said.

As soon as I gave my name, a beefy officer threw me to the floor. In that split second, I thought: If this was how they were going to respond when I gave a correct answer, what would they do if, in my nervousness, I said something that wasn't accurate? Three of them jumped on top of me. They dug their knees into my neck and back as they put the handcuffs on. To make sure I knew who was in control, they dragged me from the front door all the way to the living room. I screamed as they pulled me across the carpet. I knew I wasn't supposed to talk unless spoken to, but I blurted out, "Ah, my chest is burning! Can you please pick me up?" One officer, perhaps as part of a good cop/bad cop routine, sat me up.

They ripped our place apart as I sat and watched from the living room, the handcuffs impeding the circulation in my wrists. They walked a dog through the entire house, and he rummaged through everything. He started in the kitchen as they took everything out of the cabinets. He jumped onto the countertops. They poured every box onto the kitchen floor. They took everything out of the refrigerator and tossed it down. They began searching our couches. They cut into some of the pillows to see if anything was hidden in there.

The officers then questioned me to see if I knew where the drugs and money were. They asked if we had any weapons in the house. I was terrified, because I had seen my roommates with guns, but I had always just kept walking. I had no idea where any of it was now. I prayed that they had taken everything out. The police searched every bedroom. They took everything out of the closets and threw it onto the floor in the middle of our rooms. It looked like a tornado had come through. I sat there in disbelief. I started to feel lightheaded, because every time I tried to adjust my body, the handcuffs dug even deeper into my wrists. I tried to figure out how I would tell my parents that I was calling them from jail in Ohio for something I hadn't done. I wondered if they would believe me when I told them it wasn't my fault.

All I could do at that point was pray that the police didn't find anything that could incriminate us. They caught my roommates around the corner, driving away. They brought them back and sat them down in the living room with me as they searched. We sat around a table, watching the police and staring at one another. I had no clue what was going on in their minds. I was just hoping they had cleared their rooms. "We've got loaded gun clips back here, but there aren't any guns," the officers said, talking to one another but watching for our reactions. If they had found the guns, they could have taken us all to jail for a long time. "We have marked bills and bags of weed in this room." Luckily, they didn't find anything in my room. I had nothing to hide, but I had no way of knowing if my roommates had stashed something behind my back.

It turned out the police had been watching us for a while, so they knew I had nothing to do with what was going on. They let me go. They let us all go that day, actually, but they came back for my roommates. They never came back for me, but for weeks, I would flinch anytime I heard the floor outside the front door creak.

After that fiasco died down, I moved in with another teammate for a semester. I ended up moving again after that, and my last roommate became one of my best friends. His name was Aaron Pitts. Aaron thought on the same level as I did. He was a leader of the team. He earned great grades. He was on track to graduate after one more season. I was always taught to change your friends if they are not on the same level as you in all areas of life. If they aren't, you can love them from afar, but they will bring you down in the long run.

Before I moved in with Aaron, I would always go over to his house and eat ramen noodles. In college, that was all we had money for. We were broke. Guys did what they had to in order to make some extra money on the side. I couldn't be mad at my old roommates for doing what they had done. I knew they had felt it was what they had to do given their circumstances. I am sure they just started off as casual smokers. People liked what they were sharing, so they started selling at a small profit, and then their racket took on a life of its own.

I was determined to have a great senior season, because it was my last year of NCAA eligibility, and my window of opportunity was closing. The time was now if I wanted to make it into the NFL. Of course, along the way I had added some extra baggage to my résumé with the drug bust in that house. Plus, I was coming from a small school, which complicated things even more. Every move I made from that point on had to be the right one. I had no margin for error. I had to improve my game as much as I could to get to the NFL. Everything I did was football-related. I worked out harder than ever before. I would go on the field by myself and run routes. I wasn't even catching a ball, just working on route running. I would stop to imagine what it would be like in the NFL. Sometimes Aaron would go out there with me. We both played wide receiver, and we would throw passes to each other. I outperformed everybody in the weight room. I broke numerous records there and on the field. We had testing days where our coach gave us chances to break records that had been held for years. There was a board that showed each record, along with the player's name and the year he had set it. I had to get my name up there. That was just the competitor in me. I wanted to make sure that when the scouts came in to talk to my coaches, they would see my name before they saw my face. I broke two weight-room records. I broke the wide receiver bench-press record, benching well over 300 pounds. I broke the hang clean record. Breaking these records was very satisfying to me, because I worked very hard to do it, and the hard work paid off.

Summer training camp started, and NFL teams rolled in left and right to speak with me. I was stunned at how many knew who I was. It wasn't as if I'd had great numbers the season before, because I had barely had the ball thrown my way. At the time, YSU wasn't a school known for putting out much NFL talent. In fact, very few players even made it into NFL training camps. The number who made a team was minuscule. The odds were against me.

A handful of NFL scouts watched practice every day. They watched every move I made. They paid attention to small things, like whether I was first in line for every drill. They wanted to see how hard I practiced. Everything at that time was about my character.

The scouts came and talked with me after practices. Sometimes they sat and watched film with me if they caught me in the stadium during the day. Of course, the first thing they asked before anything football-related was, "What happened in that house last year?" I had to be honest with them, because they had a sheet with every significant detail about me dating back to my birth. "I just didn't feel like moving in the middle of a semester," I tried to reason with them. "You know how tough it is balancing academics and sports. You try to avoid all other distractions." One scout countered with, "Did you know what was going on before the police came to the house?" I told them, "I sort of did, but I guess I never took the time to consider the magnitude of the situation. I've seen drug dealing take place on a daily basis since I was in middle school. I guess I've just become desensitized to it. I did purposely keep my distance from their racket, which is why I am sitting here talking with you today and not staring at the walls of some jail cell." The NFL works closely with the FBI. If I had been dishonest, it wouldn't have gotten me anywhere. NFL scouts meet all sorts in the business, and they make their living on being able to sense a con in seconds.

Going into my senior season, I also started to receive calls from agents. This was all very new to me. I didn't know what to look for or what to say to them when they called. I received calls from area codes I had never seen in my life. I didn't know how the process worked, but I quickly figured it out. The agents get a list from the NFL every year of players they should look out for. The list includes all college players and their rankings. It has a projection of where the NFL thinks you will be drafted based on your junior season or junior combine. They rank based on potential.

The agents began calling me multiple times a day. They would tell me how much they could do for me. They would run off a list of players they already had in the NFL. In most cases, hearing the big names would lure a player to an agent. But I didn't want to go with a big-name agent, because I was coming from a small school. I had heard bad things about agents and how they stopped working for you once they signed you. They stopped working for you if you got hurt or if they thought you wouldn't make them any more money. If I went with a big-name guy, I knew that would happen at some point in my career, because those agents have no reason not to overload their client lists with hundreds of star athletes.

I wanted to narrow my search down before the season in order to concentrate on the more important things once camp and practices started. I narrowed it down to five candidates. Most of them grossly exaggerated where they could get me drafted, but I saw right through them. They offered me watches, phones, and women who would take me out for a night on the town. But if I had been caught accepting anything at that point, I wouldn't have been able to play that season under NCAA rules. While the agents went down their list of perks for signing with them, I went down my list crossing their names off.

I brought the final two candidates to visit my family before I went back to school for camp. They came to my parents' houses to sit down and talk about the business. They showed us brochures highlighting their past accomplishments. They told me where they thought I could be drafted and what I had to do. They were being salesmen. They were selling themselves to my family and to me because that's how they make their money. And that's what it's all about.

After those meetings, I decided which agent I was going to sign with, but I couldn't finalize anything until after the season. That waiting period was helpful: The amount of sincere attention each agent gave me throughout the season reassured me in my decision.

I went into my senior season strong. Once again, my teammates made me a captain. I had now been voted captain everywhere I had played. Once again, the guys looked up to me not because of my words, but because of my actions. They saw how much attention I was getting from coaches, scouts, and agents, and they wanted the same buzz. They wanted to do everything I did. They would tell me how they looked up to me, and that I was a lock to make it to the NFL. I didn't do too much yelling or try to get the team amped up. I was probably the quietest of the four captains. I let my actions speak for themselves. I showed my teammates hard work and consistency. I showed them what I thought was the way to become their best. They could see the results in their game when they did the things I did. Some asked me what my secret was. *It's easy,* I would think, *just walk like you talk.* But my answer to them was always a simple smile.

I tore my quad tendon during the fourth game of the season. In addition to being one of the starting wide receivers, I was also our team's punt returner, and while I was catching a punt, one of my teammates ran directly into my knee. I didn't think much of it until the next day, when I woke up to shooting pain. I could hardly walk and couldn't bend my leg at all, so I was consigned to limping everywhere. I couldn't sit with my leg bent for more than five minutes. I had to sleep with it straight. Every time we flew as a team, I had to sit in an aisle seat so that I could straighten my leg. I was in constant pain, and I began to look very slow on film. I lost the ability to burst out on the field. I could hardly make cuts. I couldn't run routes because I couldn't put pressure on my knee. Every time I tried to plant and cut, the pain won. It caused a lot of doubt in my mind, as well as the scouts'.

But I still played every snap in practice and games. I had to, because the scouts were coming to watch me, and I didn't want them to lose interest. It was beyond difficult to hide the pain. There were times when scouts came to see me practice and I looked horrible. I was trying to convince everyone around me that I was fine, when I should have been convincing myself that I needed to step away from the action to heal. I got into a fight one practice after a guy took a cheap shot at me. The pain instantly shot through my knee. He was trying to show off in front of the scout himself, but I didn't care. We fought right in front of the Carolina Panthers' scout.

I knew I had to get my knee looked at, because it was hurting my potential draft stock. But every time I went to the trainers, they told me it was just tendonitis, followed by the universal prescription for all pains: "Put ice on it." They did small exercises to try to strengthen it, but that never worked. I grew tired of going to see them early every morning just to get the same runaround. My knee was swollen for the rest of the year. I played the whole season in pain. It got worse every week, but I was determined not to let it stop me. I also didn't want to see a doctor, because he might force me to sit out the rest of the season. Every time I went to the training room, I would tell them, "I don't think this is tendonitis. It hurts way too much." And on top of all the pain I was in, we still didn't win the games we should have been winning. The season just dragged on.

Even so, I broke the school record for the most catches in a season. I had a great year despite the injury, ending with six touchdowns, 790 yards, and 77 catches. I could have gone double digits in touchdowns if it hadn't been for my knee. I knew that after the season, I would finally be able to get it looked at by a specialist.

Despite my contributions, we finished that season winning only five games. I hated to lose. I hated the feeling of losing more than I liked the feeling of winning. I expected to win, so that feeling was normal for me; there was nothing to celebrate. After losing, though, I would get a sick feeling in my stomach. I would look around the locker room at my teammates, and they would be laughing and playing as if it were okay to lose. It had the feeling of a funeral: a few people torn up over the loss, and the rest making lame jokes to avoid facing reality.

I grew tired of talking to them about their commitment to the team. There was only one reason we didn't win at YSU. We didn't win because we never became a family. Everyone was kicking one another's back behind closed doors. Everyone was saying that the coaches were inept and that their play-calling sucked. The vast majority of the team was solely focused on making it to the NFL, but they weren't having good college careers. At Lackawanna, we had won games because we had always come together as a team, no matter what the obstacle. We partied together. We ate together. We got in trouble together. If a fight broke out, we always had one another's back, as if we were brothers. When we got on the field, trust came easily. There was never any doubt. We weren't scared to let a teammate know when he was messing up. Everyone was a leader, no matter who the captain was. We knew when something should be said, but we never overstepped our boundaries or tried to be above the true captains. There was a respect factor. The best teams in every sport have that. The best businesses have that, as well.

At Lackawanna, we didn't have the most talented team, but we still won. Beating a team that is better than yours on paper is the ultimate feeling in sports. It means that you dug deeper. We didn't have that type of drive at YSU, and it was destroying me. I went through two long years on a clique-filled team that never gelled. I went through two long years on a team filled with nice guys — guys who didn't have the killer instinct. They didn't have what it took to succeed in this business.

I was happy to finish my college career. It was finally time to move on. I did have some fear, of course, as I was unsure of my future. I had played organized football since I was seven, and not knowing if I would ever play in a game again terrified me. Football was obviously a big part of who I was then, and it will always be. Football is part of my identity.

During my years in Youngstown, people always told me I was weird. I didn't feel like I was weird; I just chose to be different from the norm because most people reminded me of ants — always in a rush, but never appearing to get much done. I didn't talk much to people while out and about on campus. I always walked around with my headphones on, and I guess that sent off a vibe that I wasn't interesting in interacting.

The truth is, if someone had asked me what I was listening to, then I really would have been labeled weird.

Like most young inner-city students, I often gravitated toward what the high-school guys were doing. This was especially so when it came to their music of choice: rap. Today, my criticism of rap is that it isn't just the music you are internalizing, but a lifestyle. This may come as a shock to you, but the overwhelming majority of rap artists today don't speak too kindly of women in their lyrics. Many even go as far as publicly calling them hoes. As for their music videos, one word comes to mind: misogynistic. Most (there are a few rap artists I listen to, like Tupac and Common, who have uplifting and philosophical lyrics) appear to have no respect for women and find it amusing to create videos degrading them. Someday, a filmmaker is going to make a documentary interviewing the mothers and daughters of these musicians who feel more powerful by humiliating women, and that filmmaker will win countless awards.

"If you have talent, you don't need to use sex, drugs, and violence to sell music." That is the line I find myself saying more often than any other when I visit schools these days to talk with at-risk students. And if you don't agree with my theory that rap is more than just music, please contact me, and I'll try to set it up so that you can tag along on one of my middle-school visits. If you have a busy schedule, let me share with you the sights and sounds I took in on my last visit to a school. Even before I reached the classroom I was to visit that day, I got a full dose of the rap mentality students had internalized as I walked the halls. There were two guys going around and double-smacking girls' behinds while they were digging through their lockers, boys who were barking out "Double Ds!" to girls who were developing faster than their peers, and one who found it amusing to walk through the hallway with a girl in a headlock. Ideas and actions have origins. So, how do you think these *sixth graders* came up with these ideas? Hopefully, that award-winning filmmaker I mentioned will do a follow-up documentary on the way inner-city boys manhandle girls on a regular basis, and we can learn something and then change something.

When I tell my friends about these school visits, they ask how I restrain myself from grabbing one of these knuckleheads and trying to be a voice of reason. Well, first off, I am a guest at these schools. As much as I would like to put an out-of-control dude in his place so he could hopefully see the error of his ways, there is a huge audience in the hallway, and rational is not the response I would expect from a student in front of peers he tries to impress every day. I do, however, throw these guys my best "your

97

actions are not cool" face, but I do it more for the girls and the on-the-fence guys, to give them a moment of relief knowing that a better way is possible.

My last comment on that topic is to urge you to avoid the knee-jerk response of blaming teachers for letting these misbehaviors take place. Aside from offering a different perspective on life to teens who want more, my second favorite part of visiting schools is hanging out with teachers.

At Lackawanna and Youngstown, I had a chip on my shoulder because I wasn't playing D1-A. I started college still listening to rap, but I didn't like the mindset it put me in. The music made me angry. It made me blame everyone else and want to lash out. But when I sat in the library doing research, my mind sometimes drifted, and it became clear that I had no one to blame for my current situation but myself. I was angry at a world that wasn't angry at me, and lashing out would only make me look uneducated — like I was back in high school, climbing out a classroom window.

So, if you had stopped me on campus at Youngstown and asked for a listen to my headphones, you would have caught a piece of the most uplifting music of our generation: gospel. Instead of listening to music that fed my anger and made me want to act on my frustrations, I turned to gospel, and it resonated with me. I felt that mind, body, spirit connection, and for the first time since the carefree days of elementary school, I found harmony within. I was battling a bit of depression because players I used to run over on the football field were playing D1-A on television, and I was going up against schools most people had never heard of. Gospel music centered me and even made me more focused on the field.

It was rare that I went out to party with my teammates. I had gone through my partying phase, had my fun, and accumulated my fair share of

98

stories, but now my eyes were on the prize. I knew I had to be different in order to make it to the NFL. Being different didn't worry me, because I was an athlete. Plus, a teacher had once told me that "the masses are asses," and that reinforced my desire to march to the beat of a different drum. I knew I had to sacrifice fun and partying in order to achieve my goals. I also didn't trust my teammates enough to go out with them in that rough area. Many people were killed at parties in Youngstown and around the Cleveland area. The few parties I did go to all ended early with fights or shootings. The clubs in Youngstown were "wack." We shifted to house parties, but they were often even more dangerous, because nobody got checked for weapons like at the club. There were always people at the parties who looked suspicious. There were always locals who started fights with people just because they were athletes or college students. (Reminder: People destroy because they can't create.) Eventually, I stopped partying altogether because I didn't feel my teammates would have my back if something happened. There was nothing they could do if someone pulled out a gun. Our locker room had a memorial to a former football player who had been killed while partying. I received that message loud and clear.

While my teammates went out, I was at home, watching sports on television while doing ab work. I was always trying to get better. I became a real junkie for the sport. I studied the people who had already made it pro so I could emulate their key attributes. I watched highlights on YouTube of guys I admired. I watched clips of old inspirational speeches in order to get pumped up to work out. I used the little money I had from a refund check to buy a medicine ball so I could work on my core while I watched television. I trained hard every day at Youngstown State. I trained because

I wasn't satisfied with just the awards I received there or the records I broke. I wasn't where I wanted to be in life. I hadn't achieved my goal of making it to the NFL. And I didn't just want to make it to the NFL. I wanted to be a household name.

During my last couple of months at YSU, the only thing I could concentrate on was the NFL. I stopped going to class. The times I did go, I was thinking about football. I also had something else on my mind: My girlfriend, Jamilah, had informed me that she was pregnant.

That was the scariest time of my life. I didn't know what to think. When my mind cleared, the first thought that terrified me was that I didn't know how to raise a child; I'd only recently figured out my own life. The second terrifying thought was that I didn't have any money. Now I had no choice but to make it to the NFL. There was no way I would let a child of mine grow up in an environment where drug deals and violent acts were commonplace. I had to go to work.

I learned a lot about myself at YSU. I was always told that a solid college education offered academic and social growth. I nearly threw my life away because I wasn't paying attention. I wanted to quit Youngstown and transfer to another school because things weren't going my way. It was only another test. I had to be strong. I had put myself in the position to be at Youngstown and not a major D1-A college. I had to persevere. I had to fight. I had to be different.

You have to be a special person to become a professional athlete. You have to be different to make it to the top level anywhere in life. Then you have to be consistently different to stay there. It is not an even playing field. There are many great athletes in the world. You have to do something that separates you from them. What separates you? What stops that coach from deciding to take the next person in the next town over you? What makes that agent decide to invest $30,000 in you? You have to find what you're good at and become better at it every day. Then you have to identify the skills you lack and become great in those as well. It's not a job if you love it. It's your craft. Perfect your craft. Become a student of the game. Be coachable. Don't substitute skill for hard work. Be great by being different!

Chapter Seven

Yoga Mats

After my senior season, I decided on my agents, a group called XAM. I signed because of the family feeling they gave me. They were also pretty young and seemed like they wanted to work hard for me. After consulting with them, we decided that the best place to train for the NFL combine would be in Sarasota, Florida. There was a trainer down there by the name of Mike Gough. My friend Eugene Monroe had been drafted the year before, and he gave rave reviews on Mike.

Mike has been training athletes for years in his small gym. He has trained many players in the NFL, but he never wanted a big gym. He kept it small so that he could give his clients the one-on-one training they needed. Most of the bigger facilities have 50 guys training at once. One mega-gym could easily have 10 first-round draft picks in one year. If you're not slotted for the top two rounds, don't bother calling them. I knew that I was projected to go in the fourth or fifth round, so I was fine keeping things simple. There were select things I had to work on, and I needed individual attention to correct them. The gym was in a warehouse no bigger than an average-size house, and it had just the right amount of equipment for the small group of guys who worked out there. It had a small piece of turf big enough for us to stretch, do some calisthenics, and push a sled. We did our on-the-field running and training at a high-school field around the corner. Florida was always warm, and it offered plenty of field space for our workouts.

Sarasota is a tranquil oasis along Florida's western coast with breathtaking keys in the distance. The city has the most relaxed feel to it, with lakes, retired people, and mobile homes everywhere. Every home looks brand new. If I had been asked, I would have moved there permanently, because it seemed like the ideal environment to raise a child. I shared a place with another guy preparing for the combine, Deji Karim, who also came from a small school (Southern Illinois University). I knew a lot about Deji because he had won big awards at the D1-AA level. He and I had the same agents, so it was economical for them to have us room together.

Our three-bedroom condo was gorgeous. It was unlike anything I had ever stayed in. It was in a gated community up the street from Mike's gym. Behind it was a huge lake. We had a screened-in balcony where we could go to relax without getting assaulted by mosquitoes. There was also a sweet Jeep in our garage for us to use to get to know the city. Everything down to the washer and dryer was amazing. I quickly got used to this lifestyle, and I knew there was only one way I could make it an everyday thing.

Our agents paid for everything from training to living expenses. We didn't have to worry about anything other than football. They were investing $10,000 to $20,000 in us for three months of training because in return they would get 3 percent of our NFL contracts before taxes. There are four quarters in a season, each with four games. After each quarter, we would be required to pay them. Agents only go after players they feel will give them a return on their investment. They kick one another in the back. Many of them are crooked. They give players money all the time. Then they tell on one another for giving players money. It's a hard business, and the players are stuck right in the middle of it.

My first day of training was not easy. The YSU season had been over for a couple of months. The playoffs at the D1-AA level went until around Christmas, but we didn't make the playoffs, which gave me time to relax and rest my knee. I didn't know where to go and get it looked at; I thought I could just rest it in the month I had off, and that would do the trick. Because of that, I was out of shape when I showed up in Florida on January 1. Coming off Christmas break was rough for me. The rest of the guys were coming from the bowl games they had played a week or two earlier, and that rattled me.

Mike Gough's workouts were the most intense I had ever experienced. I am sort of forced to say that because I threw up on the first day of training. Mike says he does that every year so players will understand what they are getting into. He had a plan for us: We had just gotten done working out, and he gave us each a protein shake to drink. We had never been given protein shakes in college, so I wasn't used to them. I drank mine down, but the shake had other plans. Mike could see in my face that I was about to throw up. He opened the door to let me out. He screamed, "Go over to the bushes!" I barely made it to the bushes before it came up. All of the guys laughed at me. They screamed, "We got one!" It was their goal to make guys throw up after workouts. It gave them satisfaction, not to mention a good laugh at our expense.

Training in Florida was unlike anything I had gone through before. When we had worked out in college, we had done a lot of heavy weightlifting. Everybody wanted to show that they were the strongest person. But when I got down to Florida, it was mostly speed training and endurance. I was focused on flexibility and core strength, which made me faster and helped prevent injuries. We worked with bands and air machines rather than just free weights. Everything we did was focused on explosion. The trainers would say, "Football is a game of explosion, so we will practice exploding in our training." The technology was amazing. I had never seen these types of machines.

One of the main things we did was to work on ways to cheat the drills at the combine. Mike had been doing this kind of training for years. He knew every way to cheat the drills. For example, before we did the vertical jump at the combine, they would test our vertical reach. Mike taught us to retract our shoulders as we reached up, which would subtract inches from the measurement. We worked on that every day. We worked on making our shoulders more flexible in order to retract more. Mike taught us tricks to take time off on each of the speed drills. He had the combine down to a science. We worked just as hard on "gaining an edge" as we did on the actual training.

Our diets were crucial in maximizing our potential. There was always food provided for us to make sure we were eating proper meals. Mike partnered with a local business that brought healthy lunches and dinners. Everything was tailored to each player's program. It was enough to make sure we were full but not eating too much. The food was always grilled or baked to cut down on salt and sugar. After a while, we got tired of it, and on weekends we would get wings or something a little tastier to eat. Mondays sucked if we didn't eat properly. Despite the intense training program, which was costing tens of thousands of dollars, some guys still drank and smoked. They still partied on the weekends. I couldn't do that, or I would feel as if I were cheating myself. I also didn't want to go through that awful feeling on Mondays.

Our schedule was rigorous. We were divided into groups of five, and each group worked out twice a day. We ran in the morning for two hours. Then we went back home, took naps, and returned in the afternoon for a lifting session. We worked out Monday, Tuesday, Thursday, and Friday. Wednesday was our yoga day. Yoga was a whole new world for me. I had never been very flexible, so it was tough during the early weeks. I had never thought about how flexibility could change my game, along with my overall feeling. In college, the coaches had never discussed it. We had only stretched before practices and lifting sessions. I am left wondering if the coaches didn't know or just didn't care about the benefits of yoga.

Mike partnered with a place across the street where we received full-body massages once a week. We usually got them on Friday, after the last workout. Those deep-tissue massages were the best after a long week of training. They were blissful and a great way to kick off a weekend of relaxation. I didn't know about the guys who came from bigger schools, but I wasn't used to all of this hospitality. A few players surprised me when they said they had done all of these things in college.

We had a doctor down in Florida who came in once a week to check on everybody. He pushed pressure points and stopped all of our aches and pains. He commented on how fast I had the potential to be based on how flexible my ankles were. He tried everything he could on my knee, from stretching to acupuncture. Earlier, I had unsuccessfully tried a magnetic treatment that was known to work for NFL players. I drove to his office an hour away in order to receive treatments. Nothing worked for me. I was willing to do anything except get an MRI, because then I would have to inform my agents. I didn't want to tell them, because I was scared they would drop me. So I went on training with a bad knee.

I killed every training session in Florida. I gave my all despite the pain. I excelled in every area except the 40-yard dash, which was something all 32 teams questioned about me. They said I was big and physical enough to play in the NFL, but they doubted my speed. "What is your long speed?" "Could you break away from the guys without getting caught?" "Could you create separation from NFL corners?" They questioned it because of my knee and how slow it made me look on film. Nobody was willing to bet on a wide receiver who couldn't run the 40-yard dash in under 4.5 seconds.

My whole time training, I kept running 4.58, 4.6, or 4.56. The closest I could get was 4.54. I got very discouraged every time I ran the 40-yard dash so Mike could see my most recent time. I lost sleep over the fact that less than a tenth of a second was keeping me off the NFL coaches' radar. I kept thinking that when I got to the combine, I would do terribly. I was terrified to run it. But I let that fear fuel me to work harder at it every day. Every time we ran, I made sure I was doing all the little things. We broke it down into parts. Some days we worked on the first 10 yards. Other times we worked on the next 20 yards. Other days we would focus on the whole 40 yards. I made sure I was breathing right. I reminded myself to take the proper steps. I had to stay low as I burst out of the blocks. I obsessively watched track clips on YouTube in hopes of uncovering some detail we had missed. It was hard, because we didn't work on it every day. We had to work on other things as well, including endurance training. But as we worked on the other drills, I kept the 40-yard dash in the back of my mind. I would break everything down at night. I would think about the things I had done well and the things I had done wrong. It consumed my thoughts.

Mike brought in Ken Dorsey to throw to us and let us know what drills we would go through at the combine. He had played at the University of Miami and in the NFL, and it was crucial for us to get feedback from someone at the level we were reaching for. He threw to the wide receivers, running backs, and tight ends, throwing the exact routes that would be at the combine. I was in a group with Deji, Victor Cruz, Andre Dixon, and Trindon Holliday. We got great work in. We pushed one another. We competed in everything. The guy who got the most-improved times during the week was more of the man than the one who got the prettiest woman's number over the weekend — we were that serious. If Victor had a good time, I insisted on beating it, because we played the same position. Trindon was in a class of his own because he was a track star. He blew our times out of the water. He was also a lot smaller than we were, standing at 5 feet, 7 inches. Even though we knew he would beat us, we still tried to get close to his times and hoped just to tie him one day. The competition made us closer and brought out the best in us. We clowned around a lot during down time, because you cannot be that intense all day long and not blow a tire.

As time went on, we had to start getting ready for the various all-star games. I was invited to the Texas vs. The Nation game in El Paso, which is the smallest of the three major college all-star games. The Texas team is made up of players who are from Texas or played college ball in Texas. The nation team is for those without roots in the Lone Star State. But a little before I planned to head west for that game, I received a late invitation to play in the Senior Bowl in Mobile, Alabama.

The Senior Bowl is the top all-star game in college football. It may sound strange, but since I can remember, I've watched the Senior Bowl with more interest than the Super Bowl. I wanted to play in that game because it showcased the future stars of the NFL. I knew if I could make it there, I would have a great shot at being drafted. I caught a break and was invited late because one person backed out at the last minute. I got down to the practice on Wednesday. Everybody else had been there since Sunday and had been practicing since Monday. I was just pumped to be playing on the same level as the guys projected to be drafted in the first few rounds. I had watched them play on television every Saturday after my games. They had primetime games every week. I saw future first-rounders like Tim Tebow, Kyle Wilson, and Sean Weatherspoon making big plays on ESPN.

There were countless NFL head coaches, front-office personnel, and scouts throughout our hotel and the practice fields. It took a great deal of discipline to walk by future Hall of Fame coaches like Tom Coughlin, Bill Belichick, and Mike Tomlin without blurting out an introduction and likely scaring them away. There were cameras and media all over. The most famous ESPN reporters were down there. Owners and general managers were there. It was the epicenter of the college football world that week, and I was right in the middle of all of it. The amount of talent and power was colossal. I had just gone from playing in front of a few thousand people every game to playing in front of a few thousand coaches, owners, and media personnel alone. And yes, I felt the pressure.

For the Senior Bowl, two NFL coaches run the two teams. The Detroit Lions' coaching staff was on our side. It was amazing to be under the tutelage of actual NFL coaches, albeit for a short time. They got right down to business every day, so there wasn't much time to be star struck. We would wake up, go to breakfast, and then have a team meeting. We would break out into positional meetings and go over the plays we were installing in practice. We would have lunch and then head to practice. After practice, the hotel we stayed in became a zoo, with media personnel and NFL scouts trying to stop us for interviews. We didn't have much time to partake in the hype, though, because we had meetings after our meetings. After dinner was the time reserved for the scouts and coaches to talk with us individually. We would meet them in the lobby of the hotel, and sometimes passing by in an elevator. They asked me the same questions, over and over, that they had asked during my last season at YSU. They wanted to see if my answers or attitude would change. We would do interviews past midnight. When we weren't doing interviews, we were expected to do autograph signings. There was no rest time. They wanted to make the schedule rigorous for us, replicating an NFL season.

Even though the schedule was tough, I loved every minute of it. The only part I didn't like was the roommate I had. I couldn't get any sleep because he snored louder than I thought a human could. He kept me up all night, and we had to be up very early. In my sleep-deprived delirium, I became 100 percent convinced that the guy who backed out had done so when he saw who his roommate was.

On the practice field, I didn't do too well. I was exhausted from the day and night before. I also let the pressure of the environment get to me. I wasn't having fun playing. I was too worried about making a mistake with everybody watching. The coaches stood on the sidelines, and it made me nervous. I dropped passes. I couldn't get off of bump-and-run coverage. I didn't look crisp running routes. My knee was killing me, which added to the stress. This was not the time to choke.

After that week, I started to receive my first media criticism. You have to be strong-minded to play in the NFL because of the love-hate relationship with the media and fans. They tried to make me feel as if I didn't belong on that level with those players. The bloggers were relentless, and they never held back. Social media made it easy for fans who saw things on television to get to me. They started to convince me that I didn't belong in the NFL. They tried to create an impression that the moment was too big for me, and I wasn't proving them wrong. I tried my hardest not to let the harsh words get to me. I decided to stop reading articles about myself. I turned off outside noise.

My family, though, would read everything, and then call to ask if I had seen what a person had written. I told them constantly not to read those things, and especially not to bring them to my attention. I just stayed in my own skin. The only thing that mattered to me was that I knew I could play. I even had to turn off my family, because I knew they were biased and couldn't offer any clarity. It was natural for them to make me feel like I was the best. But I just wanted to play. I ended a disappointing Senior Bowl week with my head held high. I knew I still had the Texas-Nation game and combine to prove myself. I headed back to Florida for a week and began preparing for the next stage.

The following week, I traveled to El Paso for the Texas-Nation Bowl. I had heard terrifying things about El Paso before I left, but I didn't mention any of it to my folks. When I arrived, I immediately felt a bad vibe. The first thing I saw on the news in the airport was about a Mexican cartel chopping off 12 people's heads and sending them back across the river that separated El Paso and Ciudad Juárez, Mexico. When I arrived at the players' hotel, we had a big security meeting. The FBI was there, and they warned us not to cross the border for any reason, because we might not make it back. The cartels in Juárez were known for capturing Americans and torturing them. It put all of us players on edge as we sat in the room listening to the FBI explain that they wouldn't be able to help us if we were captured. It made me wonder why we were having the game in El Paso when Texas is so big.

On the field, I felt pressure to put on a much better performance than I had at the Senior Bowl, because the same scouts and media personnel were there. This game was made up of players who were on the fence when it came to being drafted. If I couldn't perform at this event, I was done. I wasn't playing in the actual game, because I had already played in the Senior Bowl. I was only practicing here to increase my stock in front of the coaches and scouts.

Every day, I came onto the practice field with a chip on my shoulder. Most of the guys knew I had played in the Senior Bowl, so they had it out for me. If we did one-on-one drills, they wanted to make sure they stuck me. If they had a chance to hit me, they wanted to make sure I didn't get back up. I loved it. I embraced the competition. It brought out the best I could give with the pain in my knee. I still hadn't informed my agents about my injury. I just kept performing. I left El Paso with my head held high, satisfied with my performance. I still needed to do something about the pain, though, because the biggest stage was right around the corner. The NFL Combine is the top of the mountain in college football. I had to bring my A game.

When I went back to Florida, I saw a doctor in the area and begged him to work some magic on my knee. He tried everything he could on it, but nothing helped. So I just had to keep pushing. Despite the pain, I had to finish my training and work on the most important elements of my game. I had to perfect my 40-yard dash. I still couldn't get the time down to what I wanted, and the combine was two weeks away. I embraced every technique Mike taught me. My numbers improved, but they showed no sign of ever breaking the 4.5-second threshold. I tortured myself with the unknowns about running the 40-yard dash in front of those who would decide my fate, and I wore down my spirit in the process.

The NFL Combine was the longest stretch of four days I have ever experienced. I had put in years of hard work to get there, but I was still a little surprised that I was even invited. In Lackawanna, we would sit and watch the combine on television. We would compare the numbers of the guys who were participating with the numbers we swore we put up. Only about 300 guys are invited every year out of the thousands who play football in college. I was honored to be one of those 300, especially given the route I'd had to take to get there.

Only a little over 200 players are drafted every year, though, so if you do the math, you quickly realize that there's still a lot of work to be done. They are giving you a ticket to the dance, but you still have to be able to strut.

The combine is a fan favorite, and commentators love pulling up old footage when an athlete they are focusing on exhibits some supernatural feat on the field. The workouts are the last part of the combine. The toughest parts happen during the three days before. Those first three days are mentally grueling. They purposely make it that way to see who cracks. I truly believe that my bumpy road in life prepared me for this test. My poor performance at the Senior Bowl also prepared me. It helped me find the fine line between being tense and intense. So, relax was what I did, and intense was what I would be.

The combine took place in Indianapolis, at Lucas Oil Stadium. Flying there, I recognized many fellow wide receivers who were on identical missions. Many of my peers were on the same flight because they, too, had been receiving special training in Florida to prepare for the ins and outs of the combine. So much for the edge I thought I would have going in. In the waiting area, not one of us made an effort to approach another and start up a friendly conversation, despite the fact that we all knew exactly who the others were because we were constantly being compared in the media. If eye contact was made, it was followed with a look of competitiveness. It was a perfect example of the economics of supply and demand: There was a much larger pool of talent than there were spots available, and the market was now open.

We landed in Indianapolis on a very cold day in February. There was a scout from the Rams calling each guy's name as we got down to the baggage claim. We collected our bags as he waited for everyone to get there.

The NFL had arranged a shuttle that took us straight to a hospital. The ride was very quiet. Everyone wore headphones and kept to himself. Once we arrived, the mental aspect of the combine began, which has a reputation for being even more exhausting than the physical trials.

First, they put us through a blood test. It was comical; there were guys who tried every excuse, from doctor's notes to watery eyes, to avoid the needle. The next test was a CAT scan of our brains to look for any trauma we might have received from the sport, foremost concussions. The test came back negative for any serious trauma, so I was cleared. Most of the concussions players sustain are never reported. The doctors told us that every time a player is hit and gets up feeling a bit off for a second, that is a concussion. When I heard that, I realized I would need more than two hands to add up the number of times I had experienced those woozy moments on the field. I had never considered being tested for brain trauma before because no coach had ever brought up the neurological wear and tear of the game — only the visible wounds.

They then took us to meet with some doctors who had lists of all the injuries we had suffered. If we had any prior injuries, we had to get a MRI. This was where I got nervous, because I didn't know if YSU had told the NFL about my knee. It turned out nobody had. They only performed an X-ray on my shoulder, because I had sprained my AC joint in college.

We left the hospital after the first round of testing and went downtown to a hotel across the street from the stadium. The hotel was very interesting because it was formerly a train station. Today, it is a historic landmark that still has old trains sitting in the middle of it. Once we arrived, we went inside to register and then to do some more tests. The first was on our legs, measuring the strength in our hamstrings and quads. This was hard for me because of my knee injury, but I still hadn't informed anyone, so I had to do the test. I pushed through the pain and received a decent score. It was obvious that one leg was stronger than the other, but no one commented on it. It took everything I had not to show how badly I was hurting. Then, finally, we went upstairs to put our belongings in our rooms. When we got to our rooms, we saw that the combine sponsor, Under Armour, had given us a load of free gear. I loved the hospitality. They gave us some time to relax before orientation and dinner.

The night of orientation, we ate dinner in the hotel's ballroom. That was the first time we saw one another all in one place. They brought in Ozzie Newsome, the general manager of the Baltimore Ravens, to speak to us, and one thing he said has always stuck with me. He told us, "This league makes $9 billion and growing every year. We don't need you. You need it." I don't think I heard anything else he said, because I was stuck on how much money this business generates. I was stuck on the fact that they really didn't need me. The way he said it made me feel like I had better come correct. There was no room for error or complacency. He said it to let us know that no NFL employee was bigger than the business. He wanted us to work hard and remain grounded, or we would quickly be replaced.

After dinner, the interview process began. They had a big room with tables set up all over. Every coach from every team were at the tables. The coaches mostly asked the same questions over and over about our lives, but some of the things they asked threw me off. For example, the wide receiver coach from the Steelers said to me, "If I walked up to you right now and punched you in the face, what would you do?" I didn't know whether I was supposed to be real or professional, so I went with my gut. I told him I would punch him in his face so hard that he wouldn't be able to do another interview that night. He laughed and said, "Great answer. I was hoping that you wouldn't let me just go over there and punch you. Then I would have thought you were a punk." They asked about my personal life and marital status. They also asked, of course, what had happened in the house in Youngstown. I was tired of answering that question.

Eventually, they tried to test our football IQ. They asked us about certain coverages, and the best plays to run against those coverages. They went through the questions fast, because we only had 15 minutes at each table. After the 15 minutes were up, a horn blew and it was time to rotate. Those were called informal interviews. They were exhausting and had us up until 1 a.m. And that was only day one.

The next morning, we had to be up at 5 to take drug tests. I was like a walking zombie, so at first it wasn't a big deal when they told me I would have to face the doctor while I urinated in a cup. Our drug tests in college hadn't been this serious. This was different, and awkward. I asked the doctor how he got used to doing this job. He just laughed it off. Then we did more tests. These had nothing to do with football; they were situational questions meant to evaluate our character. They were as simple as, "If you saw someone steal $100, would you tell or would you walk away like nothing happened?" I felt like a child answering these types of questions. Then we did a concussion test, which checked our memory. They gave us five to seven words that we had to remember and repeat back. Then they gave us numbers in different orders, and then patterns to remember. After we were

117

done with those groups of numbers, patterns, and shapes, they sneakily asked us to recall the very first set of words we heard.

Once all of that was done, we walked over to the stadium, which was amazing to me. Coming from a small school, I had never seen a stadium like this one. There were over 80,000 seats in the immaculate dome. They took us downstairs, where there were big rooms set up with six teams in each one. Each team had at least five doctors and trainers. They sat around long, boardroom-meeting tables, plugging data into their laptops.

I was nervous when I walked into the first room. When I sat down in the middle, someone walked up to me and yelled out my name and all of my prior injuries. Every doctor then approached me. The whole experience had a degrading feel, like it was the 1800s in the Deep South and I was on an auction block. They focused especially on the injuries, poking and pulling at them repeatedly while one of the doctors stared at my face to see if I was in pain. They felt around, focusing on my knees, as they did with most guys. They concentrated especially on the ligaments that hold the knee together. They didn't know about my quad tendon issue, and they didn't pick up on it. One doctor said that I needed two more MRIs, which happened to many players, so I went back to the hospital. That tacked on two more hours to the process.

Before I returned to the hospital, they took us into another room for eye exams and neurological exams. They were also giving us the results of the blood work we had done the first day. I still hadn't told anyone about my kidney disease, and I had no doubt that it would be revealed now. I went into a room with the Dallas Cowboys' trainers and doctors, and one of them read my paperwork. He went and showed another doctor. I began to get scared. "Have you ever seen a kidney specialist?" he asked. I told him that I had a doctor at home in New Jersey. "You are going to have to go home and see him, because these results don't look too good," he told me. "Your creatinine level is very high, and personally, I am not comfortable with it. Most team doctors will probably come back and say the same thing as me." As he was single-handedly destroying my dreams in a matter-of-fact tone that felt more appropriate for a car accident, my heart dropped. The combine was far from over, though, so I had to stay focused on the tasks at hand.

The next thing I had to do was take the Wonderlic Test, another IQ test, which consisted of basic math and reading questions. Even though the questions were easy, I hadn't gone over that stuff since high school. We had to answer 50 questions in just 12 minutes. I had heard of guys getting bad scores on the test, and I could see why. That time flew by.

After the long medical process, we went back to the stadium for dinner and more interviews. Some teams called players personally into hotel rooms they had set up. These were teams that were very interested in you and wanted more than the 15 minutes first allotted. These were called formal interviews. The players who were projected to be higher-round picks had more formal visits than others. I only had one, with Buffalo. I was eager to see how it compared to what I had heard in Sarasota. It ended up being a lot more intense than I had anticipated.

There were a lot more people in the room than I had expected, to start with. The Bills' head coach, general manager, scouts, and position coaches were all in attendance. Team owners are often in the room as well, but not in this case. It was very nerve-racking, because I was the only player in the room and they put me on the spot; it was the ultimate interview. They

119

sat there staring at me with the most serious looks on their faces. They watched film with me and asked about some of the plays I had made in college. They asked me to name the plays we had run and the defenses we had gone against. Then they sent me up to a dry-erase board and asked me to draw up plays and name them. They drew up a defense and asked how I would attack that coverage. I blurted out a random name of a play. They could tell I didn't know it, because they asked me for details. I walked out of there feeling like I had messed that interview up, but I figured a lot of my competition had done the same.

The next day, we had our on-the-field drills. This was the day I had been waiting for since I was a kid. I felt more relaxed now that the mental and medical testing were done. I was hoping we would do the 40-yard dash first, because as the day went on, my knee would get weaker. As I arrived at the stadium that morning, my concentration was at an all-time high. I walked in with my headphones on, listening to gospel music to get ready. We walked out onto the field under the bright lights in the dome. I looked around in amazement as my dream shifted to reality. I sat down on the field and began stretching my legs. There were guys all around me doing their own warm-ups. Some were running, while others were stretching. I tuned everyone out completely. We were split into groups, and my prayers were answered: Mine was told to head over to the 40-yard dash.

I walked over to the area where we had to do our sprints and looked up at all the scouts sitting in the stands with their stopwatches. My nervousness instantly kicked in. I wondered if all my time and effort in Sarasota would make a difference. Players were called up in alphabetical order by last name, and since I was in the middle of the pack, I had a little more time to warm up and, more importantly, to take note of idiosyncrasies in the starter's tone or routine. I wanted to see if I could pick up on any patterns that might allow me to anticipate the start and explode a split second early. The closer they got to me, the more nervous I got. Then my name and number were called on the loudspeaker. I walked up to the starting line, focused on my breathing and the way I had been practicing for weeks. I looked down the line and said a quick prayer in my head. I took another glance at the starter as I got down into my starting stance. I took my mark and got set. I put my off hand up and took off. There was a coach standing on the side with a whistle to stop me if I messed up — if I stumbled out of the blocks, or wasn't in my stance long enough for them to register my time. The moment I burst out of the block, the whistle rang in my ear.

I turned around and walked back to the starting point. I had a good chuckle over messing up, reminding myself to be intense and not tense. I got back down into my stance. I had to get it right this time. I took my mark, got set, and then I exploded. My mechanics were perfect, but I felt like I was moving too slowly. As I pushed harder to finish the last 10 yards, I thought my time would be the same as before Sarasota, maybe worse. I crossed the finish line and turned the jets off. I looked around for a sign from anyone, but nobody seemed to be checking me out; and all this time I had been concerned that *too many* people would be observing my dash. All I could do was wait for the bad news. I walked slowly back to my bag to check my phone, all the while dissecting my run. There was a three-digit text message waiting for me. 4.46. My eyes lit up. I had never run that fast in my life. I had relied on muscle memory to carry me through while avoiding any distractions, and my brain must have treated me to a well-deserved adrenaline rush.

I quickly came back to my senses, because I had to run once more. Like a robot, I followed the exact same routine to get in the zone. I got down in my stance, got set, and took off. The run felt identical to the first. I waited for my results again, praying that my first time, a personal record, hadn't been due to the timekeeper's finger twitch. I went back over to my bag and checked my phone. 4.49. Weeks of intense training, all for less than a tenth of a second shaved off my time. And it was all worth it.

I was ecstatic to the point that I didn't care about the rest of the events. I sat down on a bench as our group waited for the next drill. I didn't say much to anybody around me. I just thought about how I had proved all the coaches wrong. I had even proved myself wrong.

I took my mind off the 40-yard dash and began preparing for the vertical jump. There were two or three scouts running every drill. They called my name. I walked up to the wall where they had placed a chart that would measure my reach. I stood with my side to the wall. I reached up and retracted my shoulder at the same time, the way I had been practicing for weeks. The scout pulled on my arm as hard as he could. After he measured my reach along with everyone else's, we got ready to jump. I changed my shoes. To get a score, I had to jump and swipe the plastic pegs coming from a stand extended in the air.

I jumped and swatted a good number of them. I felt I had made a good mark. The scout informed me that I had jumped 41.5 inches. I was happy but felt I could do better. I watched the other guys averaging in the 30s, and I wanted to blow their scores out of the water. On my second jump,

I leaned back a little bit, and when I went to swipe the plastic pieces, I missed them all. I was easily an inch higher than I had been the first time, but when I asked if I could jump again, they told me I couldn't. I had to live with that first score.

The next drill was the long jump, where I would give my worst performance during the combine. For some reason, I could jump high in the air, but I couldn't explode straight out. It didn't help that I had aggravated my knee during the vertical jump. Now every drill I did would be compromised. I still had to do the three-cone drill, the pro agility drill, and the 60-yard shuttle. Every time I had to change directions, I felt pain in my knee. The pain became more intense with each drill. I pushed through it, just as I had been doing since I first hurt myself. I couldn't let that pain stop me.

I ended up placing in the top 10 at my position in every event; in some events I was in the top five. All the receivers in my group were guys whom I had watched on television, and I outperformed them.

We then had to perform our on-the-field drills, like the Gauntlet. We had to run every route of the NFL route tree while the quarterbacks threw us the ball. Most of the NFL wide receiver, quarterback, and running back coaches were down there with us. This was the time to show off and prove what we could do on the field. I caught most of the passes I could catch. Some of the balls thrown to me were terrible passes. There was nothing I could do about those. I ran every route as sharply as I could while dealing with the escalating pain. I still felt like I was tops, but I was ready for the day to be over. I was ready to get back home and finally get my knee taken care of.

As the route drills ended, so did my combine. I had put on a great performance. I was proud of myself as I boarded the bus back to the airport. I sat on the bus and thought about everything I had done on the field. I had two skeletons in my closet that I had to get rid of. I had a bad knee and a kidney disease that very few people knew about. These ailments weighed on me, because I knew things would only get worse if I didn't get them taken care of. The only way I could do that was by telling my agents. I needed to be straight with them before they heard it from the teams. It was time for me to step up, and hope my injured knee didn't let me down.

Chapter Eight

Can't Make the Club in the Tub

My experience with the NFL started off as my life has always been: Nothing was handed to me. I had a fourth-round draft grade. That meant I was projected to be drafted anywhere from the fourth round to the seventh round. There is a huge difference: Each round that passes means a significant drop in pay for your first contract. I thought I had the goods to be drafted as high as the fourth round, or maybe even to sneak in as a very late third-round pick. I thought I had proved myself in college. I felt I had done enough at the combine for the NFL teams to take a shot on me. I never thought it would work out the way it did.

During the weeks leading up to the draft, I started to lose momentum because of my kidney disease. It had never affected me while I was playing, but I started to receive calls from teams saying that they might be taking me off their draft boards because they "had concerns." My condition had come to light at the combine, and there was nothing I could do. My agents were blindsided when the teams started calling, and I felt guilty for not having informed them before signing a contract with them. They called to ask me what was going on. I told them that I had been dealing with this for years, and that it had never affected me for a single second on or off the field.

We immediately went into cleanup mode. I went to see a doctor back in New Jersey. He saw nothing of major concern and was happy to write a letter stating that I was cleared to play. The letter helped with some teams, but most had already made up their minds.

125

Most of the teams' doctors simply were not comfortable with my disease. I was starting to get scared. One of my agents would call every day and let me know what the teams were saying. I would sit on the other end of the phone in disbelief. I couldn't believe everything was slipping away. I had put in so much hard work and outperformed most of my competition at the highest level. It would have been easier to deal with if it was a mistake I had made, like getting caught up in the drug bust, had caused me to fall just short of an NFL career, but when you've been straight for so long and things still don't go your way, you lose a lot of sleep at night.

I lay in bed for hours wondering if I would be drafted. I wondered if I would ever play again. What was I going to do if I couldn't play anymore? I had a son on the way. How was I going to take care of him?

My agents kept saying that everything would be okay, but I didn't believe them. I turned out to be right. I think they were scared as well, given the money they had invested in me. They didn't think they would get it back. They had spent $20,000, so I really couldn't blame them for being nervous. I hadn't told them about my kidney condition — or my knee injury, which I still hadn't gotten looked at — in the beginning precisely because they wouldn't have taken me. I had been afraid to mention anything to anyone because the information might get back to a team, and then nobody would want me.

Draft week approached, and I became more and more nervous. Of the 32 teams in the NFL, 25 called and asked about my disease. The other seven wanted extra testing done to make sure I was okay to play. Seemingly overnight, I had become a long shot at being drafted. If I was drafted, my agents said it would be in the sixth or seventh round. There was nothing I could do but pray that one team would take a chance on me. I knew I was good enough.

The big day arrived. Most of the fellow college ballers I had kept in touch with were lighting up social media with excited comments and predictions. I stayed away from Facebook, Twitter, and the like because deep down, I was dreading the outcome of the day. I had a cookout, while most guys threw draft parties and were posting photos before the first pick was even announced. I would not recommend having a draft party, and especially posting photos from it, because there are just too many variables. Plus, fake calls go out from time to time, and people celebrate and tweet and are left crushed when someone else is called in what someone claimed was their spot. A few of my relatives got carried away with cookout invites, and more than triple the number of people I had expected showed up at my dad's house to hear my name called during the draft. My father had put together this big event for me with home-cooked food, drinks, and a deejay. My friends and family came in from out of town to watch.

I sat in my father's family room with some relatives and watched a few friends on television strike first-round gold. Everyone else mixed and mingled out back. As time went on, people would peek into the house to see what was going on. They would ask if anything had happened yet. Then they would ask why not. My heart sank more and more. I sat and watched as round after round went by, and my name was not called. It was painful to see all of the guys I had outperformed over the past few weeks get drafted before me. I could understand the guys who had put up solid numbers at major bowl games and been projected higher, but I couldn't understand how players I had never heard of could go before I did. I was happy for them, but hurt. These guys were not better than me.

Three teams called me at the start of the sixth round, and they all had the same message: "If you are not taken before our next turn comes up, we are going to draft you." Each team sounded sincere, so everyone around me started to celebrate, against my wishes. They thought we were finally going to hear my name called on television.

Kansas City told me they would take me in the sixth round. They never did. Buffalo told me they would draft me in the seventh round. I guess they forgot. The New York Giants, my last hope, told me the same thing. I watched as the last pick, nicknamed Mr. Irrelevant, was chosen. Apparently, even Mr. Irrelevant was better than me. I had just watched the entire NFL draft go by, and it was as if I didn't exist. I felt lost. All of my friends had watched, too, and I was hurt and embarrassed. I had dreamed my whole life about hearing my name called. I had put so much hard work into this.

By the final rounds, I didn't want to be drafted. I wanted to go as a free agent so that I could pick where I wanted to play and live. I wanted to be able to choose the best place for me to make a team. NFL teams usually draft players in the late rounds with no intention of keeping them. Guys will be drafted to a team that is stacked at their position, where they have no chance to make the roster.

My agents called and told me to sit tight. They said we would receive some calls shortly from teams that wanted to sign me as an undrafted free agent.

The first call came from Buffalo. My agents told me not to give them an answer right away, but to wait and see what other teams would call. The

Giants called me right after that. I was so excited. I had rooted for the Giants my whole life. It had always been my dream to play for them, and if I did, I would be able to play close to home, in front of my family and friends.

I didn't have much time to make a decision. I thought about the depth the Giants had at the wide receiver spot. They had a lot of guys they liked and played frequently. The Bills, by contrast, didn't have much depth there. So my agents and I decided to go with the Bills. It was hard to turn my home team down, but I had to play the percentages.

My agents informed the Bills that I would be coming to play for them. The team then called me for flight information to get me up to Buffalo for rookie mini-camp. I was so nervous when they called that I couldn't remember my Social Security number. The personnel guy on the other end of the phone told me to calm down. I relaxed and got him the proper information.

Then I went into the back yard and told my family and friends that I had just signed a contract with the Bills. Everyone was happy for me, but a few people made awkward comments about how the day would have been more memorable if I had been drafted. *No kidding*, I thought, but I partied as if I had been, because I had a verbal commitment from an NFL team that wanted me. Now it was time to prove the whole league wrong. I had to prove the Bills wrong, as well, for not having drafted me. It was time to fight as I always had, because I still wasn't where I wanted to be.

Because I hadn't been drafted, I had to sign the basic rookie contract: three years at $1.3 million, the league minimum. My signing bonus was $10,000. It was nothing compared with guys who had been drafted and signed for millions. I had started from the bottom in Plainfield, New Jersey, and I was now at the bottom in the NFL.

And I still had to make the team. The NFL is one of the most disloyal businesses in the world. I started to believe that the Bills had signed me with no intention of keeping me on the roster, but simply to bring in another body for their veterans to beat up on during camp. I would have to earn my spot and my money, just as I'd had to at Lackawanna and YSU.

Rookie mini-camp began a week after the draft. I flew into Buffalo, and the Bills' player personnel guy, Paul Lancaster, picked me up from the airport. We chatted during the 15-minute ride to Ralph Wilson Stadium. I took it as a good sign that I would be playing at a stadium named after a person who had made a contribution to the sport, and not a bank or ketchup company. Lancaster and I talked about what it was going to be like for me. He was honest in telling me how hard I would have to work and how difficult it was going to be.

We arrived at the stadium, and it was time to meet all of my potential teammates and coaches. I went straight into the training room to handle paperwork and get my physical. After the physicals, they sent us new guys into the players' lounge, where all of the rookies were watching television and sitting on the couches. I could feel the nervousness and tension in the air. Everyone knew we would be competing with one another for the next couple of days. Mostly, everyone had headphones on. As on the plane ride to the combine, there wasn't much conversing going on. Too many oversize egos in one room made me feel awkward.

Three other rookie wide receivers came in with me. We were all undrafted or mid- to late-round picks. We all had to learn together. We became very close from day one because we had come in the same way. But being friends off the field didn't stop us from doing what we had to on the field. The four of us were competing for one spot. I kept that in the back of my mind. I wasn't going home. I am sure they felt the same way.

The coaches handed us the playbook. It looked like a bible for football players. It was a huge binder with hundreds of plays and formations. I had never seen anything like it. I thought to myself, "They can't be serious. This is too much." I had to get ready to study hard every day, because in the NFL, the playbook is everything. If I couldn't keep up with the rest of the guys mentally, the coaches wouldn't care what I could do physically.

We immediately got to work on learning the playbook. We installed 20 plays a day. It was very stressful: We had to learn the plays in the morning before practice and know them when we got on the field in the afternoon. The next day, we would have to remember the plays from the day before and learn 20 more. I studied every night as if I were back in college, cramming for finals week. I took as many notes as I could. The coaches ran through plays in meetings so fast that I sometimes missed things, but I was afraid to raise my hand. They would make the smallest changes to a play, and if you weren't listening, you were bound to do something wrong on the field.

I had a hard time keeping up in the beginning, and I botched my fair share of plays. As soon as I thought I had it right, they would put in audibles or hot routes. Those little changes they made in meetings, which I thought I could just wing it on, would have a big impact on everything we were running. Most guys believed that they screwed with our heads on purpose to see if we could handle the pressures of the season, when they might throw anything at us during a game and we would be expected to pick it up on the fly. Every time I went on the field, my coach would yell at me for doing something wrong. I would line up in the wrong place. I would run the wrong route. I wouldn't have enough depth on the route. Sometimes they would call a play in the huddle, and I would just freeze because I had no clue where to go or what route to run. I felt as if I were running around out there with a blinking question mark over my head. The head coach would yell, "Get him out of there!" If you made too many mistakes, you would have to sit out for the rest of practice so your blunders could sink in. Undrafted players don't get many chances to be on the field, and I wasn't making the most of my limited opportunities.

I quickly learned that NFL coaches take most things for granted. They didn't break down the fundamentals or nuances of the game. They didn't teach us how to be better players. They rarely corrected our bad tendencies or taught us different approaches. They might say something in the film room about what we needed to improve on, but they never actually taught us on the field. They expected us to know everything, because this was the NFL. We were expected to have the highest set of skills mastered. The only thing they taught was the playbook. They also threw us under the bus if something went wrong. If we messed up on a play and they had forgotten to teach us that play in the meeting, it was still our fault. They claimed that they would reteach it at the next meeting, but that never happened. The coaches were trying to cover themselves as well, because they were just as expendable as the players if they didn't produce.

During the second day of rookie camp, I strained my hamstring. I lined up to run a route during a one-on-one drill, and as soon as I took off, I felt it tighten up to the point that I couldn't run anymore. I was forced to sit out and get treatment. I hated sitting on the sidelines, watching the other guys earn positions.

One of the first things the coaches said to us was that we could prevent injuries like this, and that most injuries just meant we weren't in shape. They loved to say, "Can't make the club in the tub." It was depressing, because I had trained a long time for this opportunity, and now I was letting it slip through my fingers. I had to sit out the rest of day two. I started to accept that I was going to be released. I called home and told my uncle I would need some help getting a job because I would be coming back soon. He yelled at me. He said he didn't want to hear that coming from me because it sounded like I was giving up. That wasn't in our family's DNA. "Keep pushing and stay strong," he ordered. "You never know what will happen." He reminded me of the hard times I had been through my whole career and life. "Why would it all of a sudden be easy?" he asked.

I quickly changed my mentality. I wasn't going to go out like this. I did everything I could do treatment-wise to get back on the field. I brought home bags of ice and machines that the trainers gave me to try to loosen my leg. I had ice on one hamstring and ice on the other knee. I was in all types of pain, but I was going to push through. I had always been a fighter. The pain was only temporary.

I practiced days three and four on a very sore hamstring. On top of that, I still had a torn tendon behind my kneecap. It was hard to stay focused while battling two injuries at the same time. It was going to take determination and grit to get through this mini-camp. I still forgot plays, but at least I was showing the coaches I had heart. That must have helped out, because they invited me back for training camp in the summer. Many players were cut after rookie camp. I was amazed to see how fast that could happen. I still didn't understand the business of football, as many rookies don't. I would soon learn.

After my first mini-camp, I returned to New Jersey and immediately searched for the best doctor to help with my knee. My high school trainer, Frank Colabella, introduced me to an orthopedic doctor in Princeton who was supposedly good with these injuries. I only had a couple of weeks before training camp started, so I had to get something done fast.

The way the doctor evaluated my knee was amazing. He examined it through an ultrasound, putting the machine directly on the spot where I told him it hurt. We watched on the monitor while he moved the machine around on my knee; it reminded me of the first time I had seen my son and heard his heartbeat. The image was white, with black holes on the screen where I had tares in the muscle. The doctor said that was the issue right there. He informed me that I was a perfect candidate for a PRP (platelet-rich plasma) procedure. I had heard of it, but I needed him to explain the details to me.

He told me he would take blood from my arm, cycle out the platelets, and inject them directly into the injury. He would use an ultrasound machine to see exactly where he was injecting the platelets. The procedure was very new, and there were mixed reviews on whether it really worked. But other professional athletes had raved about the results, and I was out of options, so I had to go with it. I was prepared to do anything to make the pain go away. I could hardly walk. I had been in pain for so long, and I needed to be able to perform to the best of my ability to make this team.

I hadn't informed my agents of what I was having done. Everything was confidential between the doctor and I. My agents had been amazing to me, but my life had always been about figuring things out on my own.

The day of the surgery, I was nervous. I didn't know what to expect. I hate needles, and the thought of them sticking a needle into my knee made me want to vomit. I didn't believe the numbing medication would help. But I was willing to do anything to make the team.

The procedure took almost an hour, including the time it took to cycle the blood. It was very interesting to sit and watch it on a screen. Frank was in the room with me; he kept making jokes and asking if I needed him to hold my hand. I told him no, that I was a big boy now. That brought a little levity into the room.

I knew the procedure would be painful, but I didn't expect it to hurt as badly as it did. The needle was huge. The doctor told me to look away, but I couldn't. He told me I would feel a pinch as he inserted the first needle to numb my knee. I cringed as I felt the needle slide in, but the pain went away almost instantly because of the anesthetic. He took the first needle out and inserted a bigger one to numb deeper inside my knee. He began moving the needle around, trying to reach as many areas as he could. My entire body tensed with the pressure of the needle. Then he took it out, and it was time for the biggest needle, the one he would use to inject the platelets.

The doctor told me that because I had so many tears in my tendons, the procedure might require a lot more platelets than normal, which would cause more pain and swelling. Frank and the nurse watched as I cringed once more. The doctor inserted the needle while watching on the ultrasound monitor. The pressure hurt badly. He kept going deeper and deeper into my leg. It felt as if he were hitting bone. I looked up at the monitor, trying to take my mind off the pain. It was intense; I could see the needle inside my knee, injecting the blood. The dark holes where I had tears instantly lit up and became white. The procedure took 10 minutes, but it seemed much longer. Every time he moved the needle, he would inject more platelets. The screen would light up, and the hole would be filled. I would then look back at my knee and see it swelling.

Finally, he pulled the needle out and said the magic words: "All right. We're done." I was in pain and couldn't bend my knee at all. I had to drive back home, but I wasn't sure how I would be able to get into the car.

I prayed that the procedure would work. I had just gone through some serious pain, and if it had been for nothing, I would probably break down. The major drawback to getting it done was that I would be down for some time. I wouldn't be able to train for a week and a half. I only had two weeks until training camp, so I was really cutting it close. Most of the players were working out in the meantime, but I couldn't. That would cost me when I went into training camp unconditioned, but I knew I had to let my leg heal 100 percent or I would be right back in the doctor's office.

That time off did me justice. My knee began to feel much better after only a couple of days. I was thrilled. I would finally be able to walk normally again and perform at my top level. When I went back to see my doctor, he evaluated my knee on the ultrasound monitor, and there were no holes in the muscle. He kept saying that it was amazing and that I had healed up faster than any patient he had ever treated. I responded, "That's the power of prayer!" He said that it wouldn't hurt anymore, but that my leg would be weak because it had been injured for so long. I would have to strengthen it back up. I thanked him for everything, and as soon as I walked out of his office, I experienced a strange sensation around my lips. I looked in a nearby window and noticed something unusual on my face: a smile.

The Bills held their training camp every year at St. John Fisher College near Rochester, an hour away from Buffalo. (NFL teams purposely hold camps far from home to make sure players are focused only on football.) The campus was very nice for a D3 school. When I arrived, the media was all over. There were reporters and cameras filming our every move. They stopped players as they walked into the dorm to ask them about their expectations for camp. At first I felt nervous, but when I realized the media only wanted to interview the stars of the team, that queasy feeling faded away. As an undrafted player, I received no love, and I wanted to change that.

In the dorm, they gave us a checklist of things we had to do in order to be fully registered for camp. I followed the rest of the guys because I had no clue what was going on. They gave us the keys to our rooms. Then we had to get physicals, which took forever for undrafted guys. We had to let the veterans go first. Everything in the NFL goes according to the number of years you have been in the league, and drafted players are higher on the ladder, as well. They all had endorsements, so they received unlimited amounts of gear. We undrafted players got one pair of cleats and a couple pairs of gloves. Everyone else could get new gear every day if they wanted. I was on the bottom rung, and I didn't like it. I wanted the perks everyone else got. I wanted to be treated like I belonged there.

Once we were all checked in, we had our first team meeting. The veterans were very relaxed. I wasn't. I didn't know what to expect. I had watched various shows on television about training camps and what they were like. I knew it wouldn't be long before the shenanigans started. The veterans couldn't let us live without picking on us. They would say it wasn't personal. They would tell us we had to do what they asked, or they would get us at some point.

Camp was a grind. Every day, from 6 a.m. until 10 p.m., we had nonstop meetings and practices. We had to do something to make it fun. The veterans got me during one of our very first meetings. We sat in the auditorium of one of the buildings at the college, and as we waited, one of the veterans yelled, "Let's get some action in here!" I had known this time would come for me at some point, but I didn't want to be the first person they called out. Despite my best wishes, they pointed at me first and then pointed to the stage. I had heard rumblings of guys taking other guys' playbooks and the keys to their cars. It was all fun and games, but if you didn't comply with tradition, that would just place a bigger target on your back. If they took my playbook, I would have to pay a $30,000 fine for losing it, which I obviously couldn't afford. I walked up to the front of the room and got up on stage. I asked them what they wanted me to do, and they told me to say a funny joke or sing a song. I went with a song because I figured there was more room there to make a fool of myself, and perhaps that would get me off their radar. I sang an old song from Boyz II Men, and they booed me off the stage before I even reached the chorus. Unfortunately, that was the first of many times the veterans would have fun at my expense.

Practices were miserable. We ran constantly at the wide receiver position. The veterans took their share of reps, but they would sit back and relax because they felt secure. It got to the point where we wanted them to take some reps because it was exhausting. We rookie wide receivers would stand off to the side and complain to one another about how tired we were while the veterans lay back in their chairs as if they were at a resort.

By the time I reported to training camp, I felt I had the playbook down. I had taken lots of notes during mini-camp and studied them at home. They wouldn't let us take the playbook outside of meetings and practice, so we had to write down as much as we could. There was a lot to write down, because playbooks consist of hundreds of plays, and each play involves different rules depending on the defense you're facing.

My problem was my conditioning. I was out of shape because I'd had the surgery done before camp. I hadn't told the coaches or trainers out of fear of being cut. I was now a pro, so they didn't care. My body hurt. Everyone's body hurt, but for me the pain was extreme. I ran plays that looked horrible on film. I would run "go routes" and catch the ball at 10 yards when I should have been 20 or 30 yards down the field. I was exhausted, and the coaches yelled at me. I had to fight through the pain every day to get back in shape quickly.

I didn't handle pain the way everyone else did. They took ice baths to shock their bodies, while I always just practiced through the pain until it went away. They also had private masseuses who came to the dorms and gave them massages. That was a luxury I couldn't afford.

I had to get used to the NFL. All of these guys were amazing. Back in college, there had been great players, too, but only a few per team. In the

NFL, the corners ran routes with me. In college, I would be wide open, and that's rare in the league, even during the preseason. There are no slackers in the NFL. The game moves very fast. It's not that the guys are faster; it's that they all have football sense and know how to anticipate what is coming before it comes. They watch film all day, every day, and they know everyone's tendencies. Back at Lackawanna and YSU, my habits had separated me from the pack, but everyone in the NFL had acquired the same mindset. That left me feeling average about my mental acuity, which had long given me my biggest edge.

The quarterbacks were no joke. They threw the ball before I came out of my break. I had to be precise on my routes. If I ran a route one yard too short or too far, it was a problem. The quarterbacks and coaches didn't like that. They blew up if I wasn't sharp with my routes. We had to be exactly where the quarterback wanted us to be when he wanted us to be there, because waiting a second longer in the pocket could get his bell rung. Sometimes I felt that the defensive backs read plays better than I did, and they would pick off my pass and go the other way for a touchdown.

The Bills had two second-round picks ahead of me whom I had to beat out in order to make the team. Training camp was unlike anything I had ever seen. There were up to 10,000 fans at every practice. They all cheered for the veterans to make the team. (I guess people like betting on sure things to boost their confidence in life.) Every time we walked onto the practice field, the fans would cheer for them and later ask for their autographs. They never wanted my autograph. The coaches gave the veterans every opportunity to make the team. My opportunities were limited as camp moved on, but it all fueled me. We could never really tell what was going on with the coaches in their private meetings. What I could tell was that they liked these guys. They gave them all of the attention. In meetings, they asked them questions all the time. Outside of meetings, they were joined at the hip. It was our responsibility to listen to what the coaches said to the veterans and learn from that. All I could do was my job and handle the things I could handle. If I worried about what the coaches were doing, it would only stress me out and crack my confidence.

The veterans also made things more stressful. After every practice, Lee Evans would make me carry his pads off the field into the locker room. There were times when Roscoe Parrish would join in the hijinks, and then I would have three helmets and three sets of shoulder pads to carry. In the meeting rooms, the veterans would give the rookies shopping lists and make us go to the store and buy them a bunch of stuff. Roscoe would always write down something like condoms just to get a laugh. I guess fooling around helped them decompress after all the hard work, and I have to say that things never got too bizarre, so I wound up enjoying the pranks myself. We needed fun to pull us together, because camp was beginning to drag out.

We practiced against one another for two weeks. Every other day, we had two practices, one with pads and one without. The days were intense, and practice began to get intense. Occasionally, fights broke out. We grew tired of seeing one another every day on and off the field. The veterans on defense would do things on purpose to get the rookies in trouble. They would tell me to slack off for a play, and if I did, they would go hard and make me look bad. The coaches came down hard on me when that happened. I couldn't let the veterans make me look foolish on film. So after I made that mistake once, I went hard all the time, despite their intimidating comments. They got mad at me, but better them than the coaches. Plus, I was there to take someone's spot. We were cool off the field, but there was always an underlying tension between us. These guys had families and children. They didn't want a rookie coming in and taking their spot. I had a child on the way, as well. I had to take their spot so I could take care of him.

Training camp switched gears as the preseason games came. It was all game preparation then, and not just practicing against ourselves.

Our first preseason game was in Washington, DC, against the Redskins. I knew I had to perform, because it was my first and possibly last NFL game. The rookies played the whole game to avoid injuries to the veterans. We played every snap on offense and special teams. It was the most physically draining day of my life. After every play, I would look over to the sidelines, exhausted. The veterans would be standing there with their hats on, eating sunflower seeds. They were relaxing while we were dying out there. That is the way the NFL works.

Our second preseason game was against the Indianapolis Colts. I came out for warm-ups with Jordan sneakers on. I didn't know the pregame dress code. The NFL has a rule that starting 90 minutes before kickoff, when things might begin to be televised, players can't be on the field wearing any brand names that haven't been approved by the NFL. Nike, Reebok, and Under Armour were the only approved brands at the time, and my Jordans didn't fall under Nike. The NFL assigns a guy at every game to monitor what players wear. He told me that he would have to fine me $5,000 if I didn't change my shoes. That was one of the first times I personally felt the business side of football.

As the preseason went on, I played very well. I made key catches. I began to make multiple tackles on special teams. I started to feel like I was gaining the coaches' confidence. The veterans told me that the coaches liked me and that I should keep doing what I was doing. They told me to make sure I stayed up on the playbook. They said they had seen many guys who were good but were released for not knowing the playbook. The head coach began to give me signs that he liked me, as well. He told me that I reminded him of Miles Austin, the Cowboys receiver, who was also undrafted. He told me that if I kept making plays, I would have a spot on the team.

I came into the NFL understanding what I had to do to make a final roster. I knew my role, and I became good at it. I knew I had to play special teams and be stellar. I made tackles all over the field. During my college and high-school years, you couldn't have paid me to run down the field to make a tackle, because there were too many headhunters back then. Now, I was having fun making tackles. It was different and challenging. Plus, it was nice to finally be on the giving end of pain.

As we went into the last couple of days of training camp, the infamous Cutdown Day drew closer. While everyone was preparing for that, I was also preparing for one of the biggest days of my life: the birth of my son.

August 24, 2010, was the happiest day of my life. Around 7 a.m., I got a call from my girlfriend's sister, telling me that my girlfriend had gone into labor in the middle of the night and my son was about to be born. I jumped out of bed in excitement, my head spinning. I didn't know whom to call or what to do. I had to get home to New Jersey for his birth, but I had no plane ticket. I called my agents, and they picked me up a $700 ticket home. I didn't care about the money. I drove the hour from Rochester to Buffalo for my flight to New York City. My dad picked me up from the airport, but he was in no rush. He took a wrong turn and started heading into Long Island. I warned him that I had better see my son born or we would have some problems.

When I got to the hospital, Jamilah was still in labor. They had given her some drugs that put her into another world. It was as if she had entered the Matrix. I kept watching the machine, and she was having contractions, but she wasn't feeling them. It was amazing.

Every time the doctors came into the room, they told us everything was okay. All of Jamilah's and my son's vital signs were fine. Then, suddenly, my son's heart rate dropped. We went into a panic. The doctors and nurses rushed in. They told us they would have to do an emergency C-section to get him out. They kicked me out while they took Jamilah into the operating room. They told me I would be able to watch him be born, but they had to prep her first. My heart raced as I waited for them to come out and say it was safe for me to enter. They gave me scrubs to put on to make sure I was sterile. Then they brought me into the room while they performed the surgery. It was an unbelievable sight.

I went up by Jamilah's head and held her hand. We couldn't see what the doctors were doing because they had the top half of her body behind a curtain. She was on so much medication that she could only feel pressure. She couldn't feel pain. As soon as they cut into her, they said our son was looking right at them, as if he had been waiting. They took him out of her belly, cut the cord, and cleaned him up. I was glad that a friend had told me beforehand that the minute a baby is born, he looks more like an

144

alien than a human, so I was able to give Jamilah a genuine, reassuring smile right after I saw our son.

When they took him out and I heard him cry for the first time, it sent chills through my body. I had created this life. I had helped put another human on this planet.

But before I could get too sentimental, they kicked me out of the room while they finished the surgery. As I walked out, I glanced at Jamilah's belly. I could see all her insides and thought I might pass out. I went back upstairs and informed everyone that our son was okay. I could finally relax.

My son, Kiion, was born right before midnight on August 24. The date was even more special because I had an older brother who was born and died August 24. His name was Kiion Jones. I never got to meet him. I always said I wanted to name my first son after my brother, and now I had. He was my brother reincarnated. My mother told me that was her baby. It was a weird feeling, him being born on that day.

I was only in New Jersey for two days. I had to get back up to Buffalo to finish training camp, because I was still trying to earn a spot on the team. Seeing Kiion born pushed me even more. I had to take care of this little person. It was go time.

Before I left the hospital, Kiion was supposed to be circumcised. The doctors came to take him just as I was leaving. The only thing I could think of was that they were about to cut off part of my son's penis. Being a first-time father, I had the worst thoughts floating around my head. I kept wondering what happens if they make a mistake — do they put it back? I was also feeling anxious because I knew that I wouldn't see him for quite a while.

In fact, I didn't get to see Kiion again until eight weeks later. Our only shared moments in those weeks were via Skype, and that was really difficult. I wanted to feel him, hug him, feed him, and hold him. I wanted to protect him. I wasn't there to change his diapers or do any of the things that a parent looks forward to doing. I didn't have any physical contact with him for the first couple months of his life, until he was cleared to fly. Especially as a first-time dad, that was painful. But I stayed the course in Buffalo because my motivation to play in the NFL had suddenly shifted: It was now more for Kiion than for myself. I was the number one variable in whether he would have a home with bullet holes or a swimming pool. *If I make a final NFL roster and sign a legit contract*, I thought, *Kiion won't ever have to go to a school with metal detectors*. I embraced my role of protector and provider.

Because of my professional commitments, I would miss Kiion's first two birthdays. Football camps were always in August, so there was no getting around it. We wanted to have his parties back home in New Jersey with all our family. I just had to miss them. I always said, "He will understand one day when he is living great. Daddy has to work in order to make that happen." I felt like a friend who had left her two children in Latin America so she could come to the United States first, get settled, and provide a better life for them away from gangs, drugs, and crime. I also thought about how this friend and her oldest daughter regularly went to counseling because her daughter had developed separation anxiety while she was away.

By the time I got back to Buffalo, we only had a couple of days left in camp. "I'm happy everything turned out great for you," the head coach,, said. "I was going to call you soon and let you know we needed you back up here. You're having a great camp and are close to making the team. You can't afford to miss any more days right now." I had to thank him and my wide receiver coach, Stan Hixon, for letting me go home to see my son. Most coaches would have seen my leaving as a lack of commitment.

"Cutdown" Day came, and all the players' nerves were unraveling. When I arrived at the stadium that morning, there were already cleaned-out lockers. We sat and waited, dreading the appearance of someone who would take us upstairs to be released from the team. The personnel guy came to get players one by one. We called him the grim reaper. Every time I saw him, my heart dropped. It was sad to see him cut guys I had become friends with over the past couple of months. I just knew he would come to get me, too. I didn't think they would release the two veterans.

But he never came to get me. They did release those two guys, and I had made the final roster.

I called my agents and gave them the great news. They were so happy for me. I called my family and let them know, as well. Everyone was ecstatic. All of my hard work, blood, sweat, and tears had finally paid off. It was like the world had lifted off my shoulders.

I made it to the NFL for one reason and it wasn't because I was talented. I made it because I worked harder than everyone else for the longest period of time. There were thousands of athletes who were more gifted. There were many athletes from my hometown who were better than me. But I had the determination to make it. I took advantage of the opportunity when it came. I made it through hard work and dedication. Now it was time to work just as hard to stay there, because you cannot get comfortable in this league.

When I was first invited to try out as a walk-on, I drove my old Jeep Cherokee six hours from Plainfield all the way up to Buffalo. It was a stick shift that showed its temperament when you asked it to switch gears. It would shut off on me all the time, and it didn't have heat or air conditioning. Sometimes smoke would come up into the car through the gear shaft. Driving it was always risky. Trusting it to get me to tryouts on time wasn't the best decision I ever made. The drive was in the middle of the summer, so I rode the entire way with the windows down, and with a case of bottled water to keep me, and possibly the car, from overheating. It got me to Buffalo that day, and so for luck, I kept that Jeep all the way until I made the team. Once I made it, I wanted to save up some money, so I kept driving it week after week, and it kept getting me where I had to go.

Around four weeks after making the team, I drove the Jeep to the stadium for a morning practice. I pulled into the parking lot, and Marshawn Lynch pulled up right beside me. It was near freezing that September day, and Marshawn stared at me from inside his Porsche truck with a look of disbelief. He laughed hysterically and said, "Please tell me that is not your ride." I had to laugh with him. "Nope. This is really my ride," I admitted in shame. We walked into the building, and he told the first guy he saw, Fred Jackson, what I was driving. Fred was the last person I wanted to know. He is the type of person who never forgets and will never let you live that joke down. They both laughed long and hard. I laughed along with them, but later that day I went to the nearest dealership and bought a GMC Yukon Denali.

My first season in the NFL was a learning experience. It usually takes guys some time to get used to playing in the NFL. During the first half of the season, I was the last wide receiver on the Bills' depth chart, so I was only on the field for kicking situations as part of special teams. I loved the fact that I was on the team, but I wanted to be able to put points on the board. I never complained about my position, though. I sat back and learned from veterans like Lee Evans, Roscoe Parrish, and Stevie Johnson. They taught me a lot about being a professional, which couldn't have been more different from college. They also taught me about the business of football.

Guys who were injured had to be in by 6 a.m. every day for treatments. We had to be in the stadium by 8 a.m., when team meetings started. They took attendance at every meeting. If you were late, you were fined. Most of the guys got there by 7:30 for breakfast. The team had a cafeteria where they laid out a huge buffet for us. We would then go into the special teams meeting. The whole team usually had to be in that meeting, as everyone played special teams. That would take an hour. Then we would break out into offensive meetings. We met with the quarterbacks and tight ends first. We would install our whole playbook for the week. Our offense changed depending on the team and the defense we were playing. Certain nuances of each play would change depending on the guy you were matched up against. We would install 20 or 30 new plays a day. That meeting would take an hour and a half. Positional meetings were next, and they ran until lunchtime. We would watch films of the team we were playing so we could see exactly what they would try to do to beat us.

149

We had about half an hour to eat lunch, get treatments, and have our ankles taped before we had to be on the practice fields. Some days, we would have to meet with the quarterback over lunch, without the coaches, just to get on the same page with him. Practice ran two and a half hours every day. Afterward, we would meet again to discuss what we had just done in practice. That was a normal workday in the NFL. We were in the stadium every day from 7 a.m. to at least 5 p.m. Even the one day we had off was typically spent in the stadium working out. We practiced and played on holidays. We had to lift weights twice a week before Thursday. We traveled on Saturdays. We played on Sundays. We would get on the plane right after the game and go home. Monday mornings, we were right back at it. We all had iPads, which we used to watch film at home. You had to watch film at home, because there was not enough time during the day at the stadium to break down a guy you were playing against. When you added up all those hours, it left you with around 45 minutes of quality time each day with your family. On the road, it was common for a teammate to speak of feeling like a useless husband or absent father. It took something more than sacrifice to keep up with a schedule like ours. It took stupidity.

The NFL commitment was vastly different from the three hours of practice and film time we put in every day in college. There, football just seemed like an extra class on our schedule. In the NFL, we ate, breathed, and slept football. In college, we played 11 or 12 games a year. In the NFL, 11 games is about the season's halfway point. We played four preseason and 16 regular-season games every year. The best teams had still more games to get through during the playoffs.

Twenty-plus games is a lot of football for anybody. We had to take care of our bodies in order to be at peak performance for each of those games. We had to do yoga and get full-body massages every week. I was a big fan of getting a full-body massage from a professional, but if someone had filmed us contorting our bodies this way and that on our yoga mats, it would have easily gotten a million hits on YouTube. We had to get into hot and cold tubs every day after practice. We had to maintain a strict diet, monitoring everything we ate and drank. There was no excuse for soft-tissue injuries like hamstrings, muscle pulls, or tears. Anything short of broken bones and *you* were doing something wrong. The coaches loved getting into our heads: "You can't make the club in the tub," they repeated. That meant if you couldn't stay healthy, you wouldn't be there long. I pushed through it my first season, and I performed very well.

Another obstacle during my first year was getting over being star struck every game. I would walk into stadiums and be amazed that I was really there. I would go out onto the field for pregame and feel overwhelmed as I looked around the stadium. I couldn't believe this class clown from Plainfield was under the bright lights. I had taken a more scenic route than most, but I was there. I would see world-famous guys on the other teams, and my first thought would be of how I could get a photograph with them. My first time in Baltimore, I was so amazed that I was playing against Ed Reed, Ray Lewis, and Terrell Suggs of the infamous Baltimore Ravens defense that I nearly forgot that each one thrived on knocking guys like me out of a game.

I had to hire a financial adviser, too. I'd heard too many stories about players' being ripped out of millions by their advisers, so I needed to get the best. My agents hooked me up with a man they had known for years, Peter Borowsky, who works at Morgan Stanley. He was very blunt and to-the-point with me, but surprisingly nice. I thought that my $17,000 a week after taxes was a lot of money until Pete listed the guys on my team who brought home $300,000 a week. That was a tough pill to swallow, because I felt I did more work than they did on an everyday basis.

Pete talked me into having a roommate my first year. Naaman Roosevelt and I got an apartment that we split for $1,000 a month apiece. Even though I felt like I was making a lot of money, I wasn't living the life I had envisioned. I couldn't just go and buy whatever I wanted. I knew my checks would only come for 17 weeks, and I would have to spread the money through the entire year. I had to make more. On the field, I was earning my $17,000 a week. But I needed to capitalize on my off-the-field time with endorsements.

I made big plays every game. Playing special teams is a hard way to earn a living in the NFL. Every day in practice, I did the dirty work. I practiced with our offense. I practiced with all of our special teams. I also had to run the plays for the defense that they expected the opposing team's offense to run. During practices, everyone had to run offense, special teams, and scout team because there were not enough guys on the roster for people to sit out portions. The stars of the team were the exception; they did some non-contact work on the sidelines. I wanted to be one of the guys who were able to stand on the side during practice to limit the wear and tear on their bodies. I desperately wanted to be a starter so that I could make a name for myself. I was never satisfied with just being a special teams guy. I realized that my performance on special teams had been a big factor in helping me make the team, but I was too much of a competitor for that. Jairus Byrd, our team's safety, asked me one day why I wasn't playing offense, because he saw I had skill. I told him I wasn't sure why I hadn't received my shot yet. He said to make sure I was ready when the time came. NFL seasons are long, he said, and with people getting banged up all the time, I would probably be getting my chance soon. It's sad, but you have to be ready to take advantage when other guys are down.

We rookies were really introduced to the business of the NFL early. Five games into the season, the team released Trent Edwards, our starting quarterback. They never sat him on the bench or anything. There was no warning. We sat in the stadium watching television one day, and it came across the ESPN bottom line that he had been released. The coaches hadn't even known it was going to happen. That call came from the top brass. That was the first cutthroat decision I had seen in the NFL, but it wouldn't be the last.

I received my shot on offense after Roscoe Parrish sustained an injury halfway through the season. I made the most of every opportunity there. I was first put in the slot position. I played double duty, remaining on special teams because I didn't have a full-time starter position. I started making big plays, and the coaches' confidence in my abilities began to grow. Lee Evans was injured after that, and I became a full-time starter on offense. I was playing alongside the great Stevie Johnson. Stevie and I had grown close over the last couple of months. We had gone through similar struggles. He had been a seventh-round draft pick a couple of years before me. This was his first year as a full-time starter as well. He had only played 12 snaps before this year. We were learning the system together, but Stevie was becoming a star in the process. I watched his moves on and off the field, hoping to learn what separated him from the pack.

After that move, I never played special teams again, because I was told I was making too many good plays on offense. I still didn't get the ball much (shocker, right?), but I was happy to be a starter who was catching a much-higher-than-average percentage of passes, because numbers are what catch coaches' eyes.

Then came a road game against the Cincinnati Bengals. I had a strong feeling on the plane ride over a couple days before the game that it would be a big moment for us. Perhaps I ate something rotten on the plane, because that feeling of optimism was quickly erased when we found ourselves down by 21 at halftime. Early in the third quarter, Stevie threw me a strange look in the huddle and said, "It's time to make plays. This is on us." His words put a mountain of pressure on me. That's when I knew my number would be called. The play was a screen up the middle to me, which we had been working on perfecting all year long. They snapped the ball, the pass was made, and the ball was secure in my grasp. I expected to get drilled a second after I caught the ball, but my teammates held their blocks perfectly, and the field opened up like the Red Sea. I caught a glimpse of the end zone, but it seemed too far away. Somewhere inside, I decided to just run and hopefully get a first down, maybe a bit more. A Bengal had tracked me down, but I anticipated his move and countered with a bigger move, and that was when I felt I could take it home. The adrenaline kicked my body into another gear, and I just took off with a burst of speed as if I were back at the combine looking to secure a solid time in the 40. Just as I was about to reach the Promised Land, one of the Bengals' safeties reached out and tripped me, because there was nothing else he could do to stop me. But I had made it. The green grass under my cleats had suddenly turned orange and black, and I had crossed the finish line.

I had always said that I would perform a celebration dance when I scored my first NFL touchdown. But the truth is, I was in shock and did a bunch of nothing. The next day, my teammates made fun of me for that in the film room. The guy I really heard from was Stevie. He was used to dancing at that point, and he said, "Jones, you're going to have to do better than that."

I suffered my first major concussion during the second-to-last game of the season, against the Patriots. My head pounded against the ground as I got hit going up for a pass. I knew something was wrong. I felt drunk and wobbly, and I could hardly move. I stood up and tried to walk forward, but I fell back. I was on the Patriots' sideline, so their trainers caught me. I had no clue what was going on. My teammate Naaman asked if I was okay. Since the cameras were always running, I responded with swag, "I caught it." All I cared about was that I had completed the play. I didn't care that I couldn't remember how I had gotten to the sidelines. I ran back over to my sideline to talk to our trainers. I was all over the place. A trainer asked me if I was all right. I nodded. I went back on the field to finish the game, but I couldn't focus on anything. I kept forgetting plays and where to line up. I had to ask guys in the huddle what plays had been called and what I should do.

Somehow, I managed to finish that game. Then they sat me out for the last game of the season. I really wanted to play, because it was an away game against the New York Jets, whose home games are actually in New

155

Jersey. I had been waiting my entire life for the opportunity to play in that stadium, but I was sidelined, because we were not playoff-bound and the coaches could afford to give me time to recover from the concussion.

At the end of the season, one of the front-office officials came to me and said, "You've played well this year." He told me not to relax, though, and to keep grinding. Without emotion, he said, "My job every day is to find someone who can do what you do, but cheaper." I didn't know how much cheaper they could get, because I was still making the NFL minimum wage. My teammates told me that I had done a great job and that I was a real team player. They told me to make sure I trained during the off-season. They said the coaches weren't going to release me, but I wanted to keep that starting spot.

It is very hard to maintain a career in the NFL. Less than 2 percent of all football players actually make a 53-man roster. It's even harder to stay on a team every year, and still more difficult when you come in undrafted like me. Nothing in the NFL is guaranteed. I took that mindset into the off-season. I trained hard twice a day, sometimes three times. I had to be careful, because I knew I could overwork my body. I trained at a facility in New Jersey called TEST in the mornings, with a bunch of guys from around the league who lived in the area. In the afternoon, I worked with my personal trainer, Claudia Ruffin. The veterans told me to slow down. They said, "This is a marathon, not a sprint. Don't try to do too much too fast." I didn't care. I was smart about the way I trained, but I had to go twice a day. I trained my body to the point where I couldn't move anymore. I trained until I threw up. I wanted to train like that so that I wouldn't experience those things during the season. I wanted to make sure that I trained harder than anyone else. I ate right. I did massage and yoga sessions every week. I wouldn't go into my second training camp out of shape as I had my first. I was on a new mission.

I went into my second camp confident that I had secured my spot on the team, and that my mission now was to secure my starting job. I arrived in Buffalo all smiles, because I knew that I had properly trained my body and was ready. Then I found out that the team had signed a veteran wide receiver, Brad Smith. Brad was known as a special teams guy. He had played with the Jets and was known for making big plays. They signed Brad the day we reported to training camp. When they signed him, it meant somebody else had to be released. I thought about who we had on the roster. I also thought about how many players the team usually kept. We had almost 10 wide receivers, and they only wanted to keep five or six. I called Stevie as I drove from Buffalo to Rochester and said, "Somebody has to go home, and I guarantee it will not be me." I always had that mindset if I felt backed into a corner. Stevie responded, "I feel you. Do your thing."

Going into the off-season, I had to make some business decisions of my own. I had become a starter and wanted to make more money off the field, because I saw guys on the team who weren't starters getting endorsements. Stevie and I had become inseparable, and he introduced me to his agent, CJ LaBoy. CJ was a great dude. He was a younger guy who worked very hard for Stevie, and I wanted someone who would work like that for me. Stevie told me multiple times to sign with CJ. He kept saying, "You might as well join the family, since you're already family." I couldn't resist the temptation. Stevie was having too much fun with CJ. I decided to part ways with my current agents. They were great people. They had done a lot for me. I just felt it was time to move in another direction.

As soon as I signed with CJ, he got right to work. I began doing things I could never have imagined. I was getting big-time interviews, being featured in magazines, and doing autograph signings with Stevie. I also scored a Nike contract, and they gave me $11,000 to spend on apparel that hadn't been released to the public. That was on the low end of what some guys got from Nike, but it satisfied my growing ego. I came from schools where we didn't have any major endorsements. At YSU and Lackawanna, we had Russell. This Nike deal meant a lot to me, and I was having fun. I traveled to different states and went to events that I would never have thought I could attend. I hung out with big-time executives from major corporations. I partied with celebrities in places like the Playboy Mansion. Every day of the week, I had access to parties with the most beautiful women from all around the world. I was living the dream.

One of the things I had done since college was network with people across the spectrum. I was always trying to enhance my personal brand off the field. Every year in the NFL, I met new people who were big-time. This year, I was meeting more than ever. I traveled from New York to California just for one lunch with a power player. I became friends with people in various industries. For me, it was about building relationships for the future. I never knew how long I would be able to play in the NFL, and I needed a back-up plan. I was told early on to take advantage of the NFL, because they were definitely taking advantage of me. I became friends with vice presidents of companies like Colgate, MTV, and VH1. My plan was to stay out of trouble, have fun, and network with as many people as I could, all while training for the season. I had become a real pro. I had to work just as hard off the field as I did on the field to get ready for life after football. I did that while simultaneously training harder than ever.

I came into training camp and played the best football I had ever played. I was determined to make the roster and secure my starting role again. I made big plays left and right. I jumped over guys and caught passes. I made highlight-reel diving catches. There was nothing anyone could do to stop me. I wanted to make every corner and safety look bad. The fans loved it. The coaches loved it. I loved it. I remember thinking, *if only ESPN aired our training camp highlights on SportsCenter*. Then the team made a big business transaction in my favor. Teams are always making moves to lower their bottom line. If one guy is playing at a certain level and making a certain salary, and another guy is playing the same but cheaper, they will trade or release the guy making more money. It's simple math. I was playing so well, they ended up trading Lee Evans and making me the starter in his place. Lee had already given me the heads up, but I hadn't believed him. It came as a shock to everyone. Lee was well loved in Buffalo. He was our team's deep threat. He was the man, and they traded him for some undrafted guy. It was ironic, because my entire career, coaches had told me I wasn't fast enough to play at a high level. Now, I was suddenly the team's deep threat.

Everyone questioned the move. The media began reporting various things about me. They talked about what I had done the year before, which wasn't much. They said I wasn't ready for the job. People sent me messages on social media stating their opinions on the team's decision and telling me I had better produce; I reminded myself that "fan" is short for "fanatic." I couldn't listen to any of the outside noise. Some of my teammates went to social media to vent about how unhappy they were, as well. That didn't sit well with me. I was going to prove I could be a top starter. I was going to dominate those teammates who had anything to say. I preferred to do my talking on the field, with my mouth closed.

As we went into the regular season, I made big plays when the ball was thrown my way, but I relived many aspects of college. My teammates were not throwing me the ball. We would watch film, and I would be wide open. The quarterback rarely looked my way. When he did, it was as if he were looking right through me. Once again, my teammates asked me why I wasn't getting passes. I said, "I don't know. I'm just doing my job out there." They lined me up in positions where I knew I wasn't getting the ball. I just ran routes to open Stevie up. They sold me during the week on how I might get the ball on specific routes if certain things happened. But the whole time, they were keyed in on Stevie. I was happy for Stevie because he was in a contract year, but he would actually tell our teammates to stop forcing the ball to him.

Plus, we weren't winning many games, and the media and fans look for scapegoats when the team isn't winning. The media portrayed it as if my performance was weak and I couldn't keep up. It was rough, because the media and most fans had no clue about the real reason I wasn't getting passes. I couldn't go out and complain, because coaches don't like big mouths; they release more guys for their attitude than for their performance. I just had to sit back and try to dismiss all the criticism. But the temptation to read what was written about me was too strong. For the first time, I started to listen to all of the chatter, and it got stuck in my mind. I started to lose confidence in myself. Once you lose that, it is hard to keep playing. Confidence powers the body just as stress destroys it.

I came to work depressed on a daily basis. And to make things worse, IgA nephropathy was starting to affect me, too. Some days I had a lot of energy, and others I was flat-out fatigued. I went through different moods as the disease played with my mind.

Because of these physical and mental vulnerabilities, I got hurt halfway through the season. I caught a bubble screen and began running up our sideline. When the defender tackled me, he rolled onto my leg. I instantly grabbed it. I tried to stand up, but I couldn't put any pressure on my leg. They carted me to the X-ray room underneath the stadium. Fortunately, the X-rays came back negative for broken bones. The next morning, I had to have an MRI, which revealed that I had a severe high-ankle sprain.

The doctors told me I would be out for a month. I put as much hard work as I had in the off-season into rehabbing my ankle. I did everything the doctors told me to do. I took machines home with me. I iced it all the time. I did pool workouts. I wanted to get back into the season to silence my critics. I missed three weeks and then came back to play against the Dallas Cowboys.

The week of the Dallas game, I practiced through pain every day. I could hardly walk after practice. I had to take anti-inflammatory drugs every day to make it through. I took Advil, Motrin, and Toradol; anything to ease the pain. These were drugs that I should not have been taking with my kidney disease, but I wasn't educated enough, and the team doctors didn't care about long-term issues. The doctors and trainers worked for the team.

161

They didn't work for the players. It was their job to get me back on the field as quickly as possible. The message from the brass was clear: Get them to play on Sunday by any means necessary. So they had their thoroughbreds pumped full of chemicals to compete in another race, and if one of us went down, the market was always full.

It was typical for nearly every player to receive pain meds for games, so much so that at times it felt like a medication line at a geriatric center. Sometimes guys wouldn't have injuries but would take the meds anyway. There would be a line in the training room of guys waiting to get pain shots. The first time I took one of those shots, of whose magic ingredients we were never informed, I felt as if I could run through a wall. I had become Superman. Unfortunately, when the drugs wore off, I was good old Clark Kent in the hospital. Right after the game, I experienced intense stomach pains, and the next moment, I couldn't move. I called Naaman and asked him to take me to the hospital. He dropped me off on his way to the club. The doctors gave me drugs to take the pain away, but they never talked about how that could affect my kidneys. They never said it was the shot before the game that had caused the pain in my stomach. I was just happy it went away, and I went on as if nothing had happened.

The next week, things got even worse. I took the shot before the game because I was in pain from practicing all week. We were down in Miami playing the Dolphins. I was blocking downfield on a run play, and one of our running backs, Fred Jackson, was tackled and rolled up on the same ankle I had injured before. Fred knew what he had done, because he grabbed me as soon as he did it. My ankle felt broken. It still hadn't healed from the first time.

162

When professional athletes get hurt, one thought shoots through their minds: *Please don't let this be a career-ending injury*. I thought I would have to have surgery and my career would be over. I lay on the field and cried as they put an air cast on my leg to keep it stable. The only thing I could think about was my son. If I couldn't play anymore, how could I take care of him? That was my biggest fear.

An MRI revealed that I hadn't broken my ankle, but I had sprained it worse. That hit ended my second season in the NFL, as the team decided to place me on the injured reserve list. That meant I was still on the team for the rest of the season and would get paid, but I couldn't come back to play even if we made it into the playoffs.

As we went into the off-season, the fans and the media were irate with me. They wanted the Bills to draft a wide receiver or sign a veteran in free agency. The whole off-season, I had to listen to reporters and fans say awful things about me. The team brought in veterans to visit during free agency, which meant they were looking for a replacement. The only thing I could do was sit at home and pray they didn't sign someone or take someone high in the draft. My family and friends would call and ask if I had seen what they were saying. I would tell them not to talk to me about it. I didn't want to hear or see any of that stuff, but it was out of my control. If you don't have thick skin, you won't be able to last in the NFL. The criticism fueled me. I had come into the NFL undrafted, so I had to prove my worth every day. It wasn't any different from what I had been going through since high school. I didn't just play with a chip on my shoulder. I lived with a stack of chips on my shoulder. It was me against the world. That's how I trained.

I trained that off-season with the same routine as the off-season prior. I was going into a contract year. CJ told me, "This is your year." He didn't care about the rumblings in the media. He had talked with team officials and knew what the deal was. He knew the team would give me another shot to prove myself. He made sure my mindset was right. "It's on you," he told me. "Let's get this money. None of these guys are better than you. Go prove it!" This was the moment when I could change my life forever. It was my time to shine. It was my time to get paid.

As we went into training camp, I knew I would have my best season ever. I was confident because of the way I had trained my mind and body. I excelled in every drill during camp. I tried to make someone look foolish on every route I ran, just as I had the previous year. Every time the ball was thrown my way, I was going to get it. For the first time in ages, I was actually enjoying practice. The Bills had drafted a younger guy, T.J. Graham, in the third round. He was a track star. The team had drafted him to be the deep threat, which I thought was my label. I couldn't let him take my starting spot.

I earned my starting spot during camp. As we went into the regular season, I played the best ball I had ever played. I caught more and more passes every game. The team would still line me up in places to free up other guys, but I had some plays designed for me, as well. I was scoring touchdowns and enjoying every game. It was the first time that had happened since Pop Warner football.

My family loved every moment of it, too. They traveled seven hours by truck, party bus, or limousine to watch every home game. They brought tailgate grills to make the game an event. It was like a vacation for them every other week. They got love from everyone in the parking lot because they cooked pounds of food and shared it all around. In their minds, they were the local celebrities. They invited people up to the family box after the games, which I wound up having to answer for each time. Everyone knew who they were. They were allowed to park wherever they wanted and pretty much do whatever they wanted, because they got the crowd amped before the game. It was a beautiful thing to know that my dad brought back the spirit of the Green Machine. Life was good, and we were all having fun.

I had a great time playing across the ball from Stevie. We had come from similar places, and many people felt we were on track to become the next dynamic duo in the league. We wanted to have fun all the time. Stevie always told me that it was about entertaining the fans. We competed on who had the better celebrations after a key first down or touchdown. I loved to do crazy dances after I caught touchdowns. I was living my dream. Every kid who plays football dreams of shining like that in the NFL.

I was having so much fun that I made a huge mistake. I got comfortable. I felt like I had made it and was well on my way to getting the contract I thought I deserved. I relaxed on the practice field and didn't play my hardest every play. I would catch a pass and stop running. I grew up running an extra 10 to 15 yards after every catch, but I'd lost that hunger. I needed a wake-up call fast, and I got it.

Coach Gailey called me one morning at 7. I missed his call, so he had my wide receiver coach track me down. When I got the call, I knew something was wrong. He told me that Coach Gailey wanted to see me in his office before the team meeting at 8 a.m. The ride into the stadium was nerve-racking. I knew I was playing great in games, but for some reason I still prayed that he wasn't about to release me. I arrived at the stadium and went straight to his office. I poked my head in slowly. He told me to come in and sit down. He put on film from a practice my first year in the league and then one from the day before. It was night and day. He asked me if I saw a difference. I saw it immediately. He told me he never wanted to see that again or I wouldn't be starting. He said I was better than that and was getting caught up in the glamor.

I was shocked that they kept practice film from that far back, but I got the message. I started balling every second of every play in practice and in games. I ran after every catch in practice. I didn't want to give Coach Gailey any reason to be mad. Practicing like that carried over into the games. We are creatures of habit, and I was done developing bad ones. I took my good habits into games and performed better than I had all year. They began designing more plays for me, and I capitalized on them. Then something went wrong.

We were beating New England at home. Stevie scored to put us up by one touchdown. Then it was my turn. I caught a pass up the middle and ran for the longest touchdown of my career. The play went almost 70 yards, but as I was running, my legs were like jelly. It felt like I was slowly sinking into the field. I was losing stamina, like I had a flat tire. Once I got to the end zone, I was so dizzy I felt as if I would pass out. Everyone was cheering, and I couldn't see anything. I ran all the way through the end zone to lean on the wall, but the fans were going crazy. They grabbed me and almost pulled me into the stands with them. As I broke loose and came back to the sideline, I couldn't breathe. The team doctors brought the oxygen tanks over to me, but that didn't help. It took a long time for my vision to come back.

I was also very sluggish for the rest of the game. I knew something was wrong, but I didn't speak up.

As the season went on, my vision got worse. It was weird, because even though I couldn't see clearly, I was playing my best football, catching everything in practices and in games. I didn't understand what was going on. I had never had problems with my eyes in the past. I decided to tell my coaches and teammates that my vision was blurry at best. They informed the trainers, and it was all downhill from there.

The trainers sent me to an eye specialist to get checked out. The first thing the doctor said was, "Your blood pressure is very high." He said he could see it through my eyes. I had never had blood pressure problems before, so this was news to me. I told him that I'd had kidney issues in the past. He suggested that I go see a nephrologist. I had to figure out why this was happening, so I went to see the team doctor first. He did some blood work, which showed that my creatinine levels, an indicator of kidney function, had skyrocketed to more than four milligrams per deciliter. They should have been in the 1.0 range. The doctor seemed uneasy when he told me. He sent me to a nephrologist right away.

The nephrologist had his own office on a different floor from my normal doctor. When I walked into his room, he was very cold. He had already seen the results of my blood tests, and he began to ask questions. My heart was racing. Then he told me that I would need a kidney transplant in the next couple of years.

My heart dropped. Tears began to form. I couldn't believe what he was saying. I could only muster one question: What was going to happen to my football career? He said that I probably had one year left to play, and then I would have to get the surgery. He said my career would end after that because I wouldn't be able to take a hit to the kidneys.

The news was shattering. I began to cry. It seemed like a dream: This man had just declared that my football career was over. He didn't have any compassion, so he called in my normal, much nicer, doctor, who tried to make me feel a little better about what was going on. He informed me that kidneys were the easiest and most common of all organs to transplant. I didn't care about that. "You're done with football" was the never-ending loop playing in my mind. He eventually calmed me down, and I left the office. As I was leaving, he told me that I could finish this season and maybe one more, but that they would have to come up with a plan to monitor my playing.

I called my mother as I walked out and broke the bad news. I trembled as I told her there was nothing I could do. I didn't know what my future held. I didn't know how I was going to take care of my son. She began crying, but I could tell she was trying to hide it. She talked to me through her tears and managed to bring a sense of calm over both of us.

Then I called my dad. He didn't have much to say. He just asked what the next steps were. I told him I had to wait until the next day to talk to the doctors again. I told him that I would be okay and that I would update him as soon as I found out what they wanted to do.

I decided to call a handful of my teammates and let them know what had happened, too. They thought I would be getting a transplant right away. I received countless text messages from everyone on the team saying that they were praying for me.

The next day came very slowly. I felt like everyone was watching me as I walked through the doors of the stadium. Everyone approached me and asked questions. I tried to keep a positive outlook and a smile on my face. When I walked into the training room, the doctors were there. They called me into the back room to give me the master plan for the rest of the season. They told me they would be putting me on medicine to control my blood pressure, which was crucial in improving kidney function. They also wanted to put me on a steroid called prednisone. They added that I had to stay hydrated; otherwise, my kidney function would get worse. And I would have to see the doctor early every Monday for the rest of the season so he could clear me for the week.

It was going to be a lot, but I was willing to do whatever I had to in order to finish the season. All I wanted to do was play. I wanted to enjoy every moment of every day for what would most likely be my last season. I didn't know when it would be over for good. I went from focusing on getting a big contract, to enjoying every practice and game, to trying to stay alive.

The first week, I had to urinate in a jug for 24 hours so that the doctors could measure the amount of protein in my urine. Walking around everywhere with this big red jug was weird. Guys at the stadium would ask about it, or make fun and say how nasty it was. Every Monday morning, I had my blood drawn. I grew tired of that, as well. I just wanted to play football.

Then there were the side effects of the drugs, which hindered me when I played. I hadn't researched them because I was still in denial. The steroids and the blood pressure medicine together caused my legs to swell up like balloons, to the point that I couldn't fit socks on. The trainers gave me different sleeves to try to reduce the swelling, but none of them worked. My legs were so big that I could push my finger all the way down to the bone and watch the indentation slowly rise, as if I'd just poked a foam pillow. Every night, the swelling decreased as I slept, but when I started to move around, it returned fast. I was scared to wear shorts. Guys on the team would make jokes about me having kankles. They didn't understand where the swelling was coming from. Every time someone saw me, they would make a comment, often ignorant and meant to hurt. I grew tired of answering the same questions. I began wearing sweatpants to avoid the pointing and snickering.

The medicine did have a bittersweet side effect — it took away all the pain from my injuries. I was able to play without feeling anything, but I had learned not to trust something that didn't feel natural. The steroids made my tendons and muscles very weak. I ended up tearing the calf muscle in the same leg as the quad tendon issue I'd had fixed three years prior. My heart was bigger than my brain, so I went on to play a few games anyway.

Everything was happening all at once. My life was falling apart. The steroids gave me mood swings. I was melancholy one minute and gleeful the next. The team began slowly moving me out of the offense. I saw less and less playing time. T.J. became the full-time starter. I hit rock bottom. I went from playing great and preparing to sign a contract, to barely playing at all. A new contract was on the back burner. I didn't even know if I could play the next year, or if anyone would want me.

One of the last games I was active for that season was against the Seattle Seahawks. We were playing them up in Toronto, Canada. Stevie and

I were scheduled to do an interview with MTV the night before the game. They had also invited us to see the Toronto Raptors game that night. We traveled by limo instead of taking the bus with the team. During the ride up to Toronto, Stevie said something that really stuck with me. "Hey, Jones. Did you ever think that all of this is happening to you for a reason? Like God has a plan. Perhaps it's bigger than football for you. Maybe football isn't what you're supposed to be doing. Keep your head up, because I think everything will be okay. Who knows, you might go on to be an inspiration for people who really need it." I stared out the window and thought about what he had just said. It was a normal thing to say to someone in my situation, but it stuck with me because Stevie never waxed philosophic. Like an older brother, he was always clowning or writing raps in his notebook. For whatever reason, it changed my outlook on life, and right then and there, the NFL wasn't such a big deal anymore.

Every day, I came into the stadium and tried to keep to my routine. I spent hours every day in the training room with an air compression machine, trying to push the swelling out of my legs. They would look good when I was done with the machine, but once I started to move, they would swell back up. One day, I came into the stadium and saw that the swelling in my ankles had become grotesque. The trainers looked at them in shock. They didn't know what to do. They went into the back room to talk about it. When you cause doctors to scratch their heads, what comes next is never good.

The Next day I was called into the executive's offices. I was informed that I would be put on the "non football injured reserve lists". Under the NFL rules, the team didn't have to pay me anymore for the rest of the season. They informed me they liked and respected me, so they were going to pay me anyway. I was however informed of why I was being placed on that list. The fact was that my kidneys were failing. Every team in sports would've reacted like that.

Mentally, I was all over the place. Thoughts of skepticism crept into my mind. Maybe the steroids, in which I was prescribed, had to do with injuring my legs. Steroids are known to make ligaments weak. I had to give everyone involved the benefit of the doubt, but I questioned everything in my mind. I took it personal even though I shouldn't have. That's how the league works, and with my creatinine hovering around 5.0 (normal levels are down in the 1 range), they were really trying to look out for me, but I didn't want to realize the fact.

The season ended, and I went into the off-season as a restricted free agent. This meant the team had to decide if they wanted to extend my contract for another year or not. It was out of my hands. Everything depended on a letter from an outside doctor. I asked the trainers in Buffalo to find me the best doctor back in New Jersey. They searched long and hard and came up with Gerald Appel, a nephrologist in New York City. I researched him, and everything I saw gave me the impression that he was the perfect fit.

He was hard to contact at first. He traveled a lot, speaking to doctors at hospitals around the world. I was determined to use all the contacts I had acquired over the years to track him down. One contact recommended that I give the NBA star Alonzo Mourning a call, because he'd had a kidney transplant done by Dr. Appel and resumed his career. I figured that if my media people in Buffalo couldn't reach Dr. Appel, then Alonzo could. In the meantime, I contacted kidney organizations to see if I could make some headway. I pretty much assembled a small army to try to track Dr. Appel down on my behalf, and then I started to wonder if hearing from too many of my people might scare him away. The same amount of work that I had put into football, I now had to put into my health. I wanted the best doctor there was, and he was it.

Dr. Appel eventually called me, and I arranged to travel to New York City on the next available flight to see him. I was shocked when I walked into his office, because the walls were covered with plaques for his many accolades in the health world. He also had pictures of celebrities and athletes whom he had worked with over the years. It was funny; he had treated many basketball players, and he looked like a child next to them. I was also shocked by how nice he was. He was nothing like the nephrologist in Buffalo. I had expected him to be cold because of how well known he was. I had expected him to talk like a big shot because of his global reach. He was nothing like that, but he was brilliant. I asked him to break my disease down as if I were a three-year-old, and that's what he did. He told me exactly what I had and what the statistics were. He showed me slides from presentations he had done over the years, which included detailed pictures of the disease's effects. He told me that IgA nephropathy was known to be rare in African-Americans. I didn't understand how I had something that was rare in blacks, especially when there was no history of kidney disease in my family.

It was time for us to get down to business. The first thing he wanted to do was draw blood. Then he told me that he wanted to do another biopsy. I dreaded this procedure; I remembered what it had been like the first time

I had it in college. He told me that two-thirds of my kidneys were scarred, and there was nothing we could do about that. He said we could use steroids to reduce the inflammation, which might lower my creatinine levels somewhat. He said it wasn't a sure thing, but we could try. He was known for getting athletes back in playing shape, so I had to listen to him.

He put me on the highest possible dose of steroids. We had to get to work fast, because I still wanted to sign that contract. My contract depended on him getting my creatinine levels back down to where the Bills felt it was safe for me to play. I hated the drugs and experienced all sorts of side effects, like depression, acne, insomnia, and overall achiness. The steroids played with my mind all the time. My son gave me confused looks when I was on them, and I've always used him as the gauge for my well-being. Like a normal child, he wanted to play all the time, but I typically felt tired or just wasn't in the mood. One time we were playing, and he kept bouncing on me. I snapped and told him to get off me and not to touch me too much. That's not something a father should ever say to his three-year-old son. I tried to explain that it wasn't me talking, but he just stared deeper into my eyes.

I endured numerous side effects from the prednisone, but I don't think any of them affected me more than the acne. My face and back made me feel as if I were going through puberty all over again. It started out like heat bumps and got worse and worse. Every day, I woke up with more and more pimples. It made me not want to be around people, because I felt like everyone stared at my face. It was embarrassing to have acne that bad at 25, but there was nothing I could do. I was already dealing with depression as a side effect, and the acne made it worse. Every time I went to the doctor, I

174

would say, "Doc, I can't deal with all this acne." Dr. Appel would reply, "It's only temporary, because of the drugs." I had to be on prednisone for months before I could totally come off it; I was on such a high dosage that they had to taper it off slowly. I would talk to my friends and family about it, and they would try to keep my confidence high, saying, "You look fine; it's really not that bad." It was obvious that they were lying.

After months of being on the drugs, my creatinine level came down a little bit. Dr. Appel wrote a letter on my behalf to the whole league stating that I was cleared to play one more season as long as I was monitored closely. He and CJ worked very hard for me. They collaborated on what should be said to team officials. CJ talked to the Bills constantly.

All I could do for the next couple of months was sit and wait. I had to wait for the Bills to make a decision on my future. I prayed the letter would persuade them to keep our relationship going.

We went through some discussions with the team about my future. They told CJ that they needed more time. A few days later, of couple of the team executives called me. They told me that they didn't want to have to let me go because I was the team's starting wide receiver, but that they weren't comfortable with my condition. As I listened, my heart dropped. I had put so much work into this season. I felt like I was so close to signing a contract with the team. I had done everything the right way. I couldn't understand why this was happening to me. I felt like my whole life was being taken away. Now I had to call my family and give them some more bad news.

When the team released me, which happened to be two weeks after I had bought a new Mercedes, I had to move out of my apartment in Buffalo. The transition was rough, because it had been home for three and a half years. I had to move everything back to New Jersey, where I knew everyone would have a litany of questions.

When I returned to New Jersey, I had no place to stay. I looked all around, but my options were almost nonexistent because of my terrible credit. I had a decent amount of money in the bank, but nobody felt comfortable getting into a contract with me — the story of my life, huh? My bad credit was mainly a result of having too much money at a young age and not taking care of the credit card and medical bills that were piling up.

Every time I wanted to make a big purchase, I had to pay in cash. When I was looking for a place for Jamilah, Kiion and me to live, it was embarrassing — just weeks ago I had been a professional athlete, and now I was a nobody. The first thing every landlord asked, just like in those commercials, was, "What's your credit score?" I went to 15 places, and they all turned me away because of my lousy credit. It got to the point where I offered to pay one year's rent in advance, and I was still turned down.

My bad credit was also a result of not paying my school loans on time. These were the same loans I'd had to take out because I hadn't done my work in high school, forcing me to attend Lackawanna and YSU on partial scholarships. My poor performance in high school was like bad mileage on a car that always lingered.

I couldn't get an apartment, so I had to move Kiion and Jamilah into an extended-stay hotel for a couple of months. It was the darkest episode I'd ever experienced, because my financial issues were coupled with my health concerns. I was still on the steroids, which left me depressed. The thought of making my family live in a small hotel room hurt my soul because I thought I had been working toward a better life for them. I felt like a failure. Kiion had no room to play or become independent. The room had a bed and a pullout couch, and it was so small that when I pulled the bed out of the couch, they touched. There was a very small kitchen and a tiny bathroom. Closet space was a joke, so bags of clothes were all over the place. I tried to make light of the situation so it wouldn't break me and had my son help me pick out an outfit from my "floor-drobe." Jamilah and Kiion slept in the bed. I slept on the pullout couch right across from them. The only things that kept me together at that time were prayer and the joy of my son. He didn't care where we stayed. He was just thrilled to be with his mommy and daddy.

The drugs took over my mind. I didn't want to speak to anyone. My son didn't understand it. He had grown up watching me on television. Whenever the Bills played, he shouted, "Daddy, look, it's your team!" I believe somewhere along the way his sharp three-year-old mind made the connection that the Bills paid our bills. He talked about the Bills and pretended to be a Bill all the time. When we watched them on Sundays, I could see his eyes dart around the screen looking for #19. I felt like I had let him down. "Daddy doesn't play for Buffalo anymore," I tried to explain through watery eyes. To which he responded with a child's favorite three-letter word: "Why?" "Because Daddy got sick. But not the kind of sick where I can give it to you or other people." Which was followed by another "Why?" His inquisitive questions hurt, because I wasn't sure if he understood my situation or my pain. I had known this conversation would eventually happen, but I had thought I had more time. I had done a lot of wrong things in my life, so maybe this was karma.

177

CJ remained optimistic. He said that I had enough solid film to make another team want me. I prayed that he was right, because the doctors had put a one-year window on my career. I ended up getting calls from 10 teams that wanted me to visit for sit-down interviews. None were keen on offering me a substantial amount of money, but I would be employed. Despite the many leads, I felt as if I had been relegated to the grocery store's bargain bin.

CJ and I lined up a few team visits. It did feel good to be wanted. I felt like my name was known throughout the league. I had received so much bad news over the past few months, and now I had something to really feel good about. My first trip was to New England. CJ and I figured that if I visited the Patriots first, it would persuade other teams to take a look.

New England showed a lot of interest in me during the recruiting process. When I got to Massachusetts, they made me feel like they wanted me. They made me feel like this was the place for me. It was just like recruiting for college. They said all the right things. The coaches were very nice to me. I met with the entire offensive staff for hours. I also had an extensive visit with the team doctors. They tested everything health-related that they could. They also called Dr. Appel. Finally, when I was done at the hospital, I met with the Patriots' head coach. I sat in his office and talked about my health. He said that I had a good chance to join the team and compete for a starting spot. He said his staff had studied me for years because I had always put up good numbers against them. He asked if I would want to be a Patriot if I passed their health exams and the money was right. I knew my fans back in Buffalo would hate me for the decision, but I couldn't pass up an opportunity to play with Tom Brady, arguably the best quarterback ever. I told Coach Belichick, "It would be an honor to play for you."

Now we had to settle on the money. I was asked to return the next day so they could work on the logistics overnight. I didn't think they would offer me anything more than a one-year contract. CJ agreed, but he focused on how it might be a chance to make a Super Bowl run. The next morning, the Patriots offered me a three-year contract with bonuses that would total about $7 million if I hit all my incentives.

I signed and shook their hands. It turned out to be a terrible decision. They signed me with no intention of keeping me. They knew I wouldn't hit my bonuses. They were treating me like an undrafted rookie. I would have to fight my way onto the team. This was nothing new. The difference was that I would be fighting for a spot on the roster while also fighting for my life.

Before reporting for mini-camp with the Patriots, I had to get another operation on my knee. Before they could do the surgery, I had to come off the large dosages of prednisone, as the steroids would delay the healing process. Dr. Appel couldn't just take me off the medicine. He had to slowly taper it down. It took weeks, which prevented me from training for camp.

One week before camp, the doctors finally decided I could have the surgery. It was called the "fast operation," and it was totally different from the first one. My knee had a large amount of scar tissue after my first PRP procedure three years prior. During the fast operation, the doctors took a probe that was like a small vacuum and stuck it into my knee to suck out the scar tissue. After that was done, they did a PRP procedure to heal it.

They usually put you under because it is very painful, but because of my kidneys, I couldn't receive general anesthesia. I had to do the whole thing awake, with only local anesthesia. I pretty much felt everything.

I went down to Princeton to see the same doctor who had done the original surgery. When I got there, the process started out the same. He drew blood from my arm and cycled out the platelets. I sat and watched as he went through the preparation process. He cleaned off my knee and blasted it with as much medication as he could. He moved the needle around and injected the anesthetic all over. It was excruciating. I knew that the procedure would hurt because even the small needle they used to numb my leg hurt. My body was tense. The doctor had to do the "fast operation" first, and he stuck the needle into my knee. We watched on the monitor as he did the entire procedure. The numbing medication seemed to do nothing. He moved the needle around inside my leg. I could feel the probe breaking up the thick scar tissue. He started to push with more force to try to get through it, and it felt as if the needle were scraping my bone. This part took about seven minutes. He then had to perform the PRP procedure to heal it.

I lay there in pain as he took one needle out of my knee and got ready to insert the next. At one point, I couldn't take it anymore and blurted out, "Doc, hurry up!" He looked shocked, as if he had forgotten I wasn't under general anesthesia. I couldn't believe I was actually conscious while getting surgery done. I was going through all of this just to play football. I thought to myself, *you're a fool*. He inserted the PRP needle and began injecting the platelets into my knee. He had to blast my entire knee. He moved the needle around while he watched on the screen. I pleaded with him to finish up. I didn't think I could tolerate the pain any longer. He finally finished and put a brace on me.

I still had to wait to heal before I could get back to training. Mini-camp for the Patriots was set to start in a week. There was nothing I could do to prepare. I just wanted the pain in my knee to go away before camp so that I could run normally again. As the week passed, I didn't really feel results from the surgery, because the dosage of steroids was still too high. Neither the Patriots nor CJ knew about the procedure. I even paid cash instead of using my insurance, because sometimes the NFL seemed like Orwell's Big Brother.

I reported to mini-camp in New England and hated it. I didn't like the whole vibe of the team. There was none of the family feel I had grown accustomed to in Buffalo. Here, football was business at all times. I didn't like the way the coaches talked to us. We were grown men, and they talked to us as if we were children. Most veterans won't take that kind of condescending treatment, but guys on the Patriots would put up with it out of fear that they would be cut. I was trying to play through major health issues, so I couldn't have cared less what any of the coaches had to say.

The coaches knew what I was dealing with, but they didn't seem to care. I knew a guy in the Atlanta Falcons' front office, and he told me how they talked about the players in the coaches' meetings. I could only imagine what the coaches in New England were saying about us behind closed doors. They smiled to our faces, but for them, it was only about winning. I was fighting for my life and trying to make some money to take care of my son at the same time. I had no respect for the coaches, nor did I want to be friendly with them. I was dealing with a lot at one time.

I had been on the steroids for months, and they made my body weak. The coaches knew about my condition and the drugs I was taking. They knew it was going to take some time for me to get back into shape. I hadn't trained in months, while the other players had been training the whole off-season. I had to sit out half of our workouts because I was so tired. I was embarrassed. I had always been someone who was in top shape, but now I couldn't even finish our training sessions.

During my short stint in New England, I had to go see the team's doctor in Boston for checkups once a week. Every Wednesday, I would make the 40-minute drive from Gillette Stadium to the doctor in downtown Boston. I also had to receive Procrit shots to correct the anemia I had been dealing with because my kidneys were failing. The anemia made me feel cold, tired, and weak all the time. The doctors up at Massachusetts General said that I could insert the needle myself every other week to save the trip, but I couldn't bring myself to do that. The one-hour trips to Boston became annoying. Some weeks I did it twice, and others I did it once.

During workouts, I didn't have the energy to keep up with my teammates. My body couldn't recover as fast as theirs did. When I got back to my hotel room after workouts, I would sleep for hours. In team meetings, I would bundle up and still be shivering. I couldn't pay attention because I was so cold and tired. The shots I received every Wednesday helped correct the anemia, but they were also known to raise blood pressure, so it was a delicate balance. The doctors had to monitor me extremely closely to make sure they weren't giving me too much.

I also started having excruciating cramps. My legs fluttered all day long, and with every step I took, a cramp threatened to take hold. In the middle of the night, they would seize me and cost me hours of sleep. Dr. Appel tried everything. He had me drink tonic water a few times a day despite the horrific taste, but nothing worked. I asked him if the cramps were normal. He said that they were a side effect of the steroids and that everyone went through them, but that most people were not engaged in a professional sport, so they weren't usually so intense. The best he could tell me was that over time, as I came off the meds, the cramps would stop.

On the field was where I felt the pain the most. Every time I went to burst into a run, my legs tightened. There was nothing I could do about it. I had to come off the steroids slowly, but I had been on them for so long, and they were really taking a toll. I wanted to stop taking them cold turkey. Every day, I had to fight that urge. I had to listen to the doctors and decrease the dosage gradually, even though I couldn't perform on the field.

I stunk it up in practice. Neither my mind nor my body was into it. From the beginning, the team had me in the back with the rookies, which made me feel disrespected. They never gave me a real chance. I couldn't perform at the top level because my body wasn't in good shape. I was also in pain because of my knee. I limped everywhere I went. In the weight room, I avoided certain exercises that would aggravate my knee. I couldn't concentrate on anything.

This offensive playbook is one of the hardest to master in the NFL. One night, I needed a mental break and chose not to study the plays. I sat in my hotel room and watched the NBA playoffs instead. In my mind, I was preparing to retire. I told my family that I hated the organization. I was just there to collect a check. I didn't want to be in New England anymore. There was no way I could last an entire season up there. My childhood dreams

183

about the NFL had been tainted by reality, and I didn't want to be part of it anymore.

It took me a long time to fully understand the business side of football, as it does most athletes. I was upset at the trainers in Buffalo and the coaches in New England for the things I thought they did wrong. I took it personally. But by the time I was contemplating retiring, I fully understood the ins and outs of the NFL. I couldn't be mad or upset at them. It wasn't personal. It never was. It was always business. I was a tool in the garage that they used. I had become too worn-out and rusty, so it was time for them to get a new one.

A couple weeks after I got home for break, the Patriots called and said they were going to release me. They said I wasn't the same player they had seen on film before they signed me. It was a business move — they released me a day before I was set to receive a $250,000 bonus. They were cutthroat. They didn't care about me, and I no longer cared about them. Honestly, I was happy they released me. I had actually been hoping they would do so before camp so that I could find somewhere else to play.

I never received one call from the coaches in New England wishing me luck, professionally or health-wise. I felt so much hate toward them, but I had to let that go, because I wanted my body to heal. I couldn't let anger get in the way of that process. Besides, I knew that was how it went in the NFL. The coaches don't care about the players. They care about themselves and winning. If you can't help them win, you are nothing to them.

The one person I respected in New England was Tom Brady. It wasn't just because of who he was or what he had done to that point, but because of how hard he worked every day to win more championships. I was impressed with the time he spent in the meeting rooms. It was remarkable how he pushed himself harder than anyone else during the workouts. In terms of speed, he's certainly below average in the league, but he beat everyone in wind sprints because during the season, he was always in top shape. He put a lot of pressure on himself and others every day to perform in workouts, in the classroom, and on the field. If you messed up a play or he didn't trust you, you wouldn't sniff the field. If you dropped a pass he had thrown, he gave you an earful. It didn't matter if it was a bad ball; he wanted you to catch it, because not all passes in the game were going to be good passes. The pressure he puts on players is what makes or breaks them. That's what makes him the best quarterback in the game, and probably the best of all time. It is his pure athleticism mixed with his mental acuity. Simply put, during the game, he is the smartest guy on the field, including the coaches.

I received a lot of interest from other teams after the Patriots released me. We talked to about 7 different teams that had interest in bringing me in. I only got the chance to visit two teams. The main focus during these visits were the medical tests. The teams wanted to know if my kidneys could hold up for a season. Right away, I fell in love with Indianapolis. One of the main executives was the nicest guy. The head coach had just gone through a battle with cancer, so he and I connected right away. They wanted me badly. I wanted them badly. If things checked out in the health department, they were going to sign me.

During my visit, they made me do a stress test. During the test, my blood pressure jumped to 250/110. I was almost at the point of having a stroke. It was crazy. That morning, the general manager had been telling me how much he wanted me, and by the afternoon, he told me the team had decided to sign someone else. I didn't have it in me to get mad anymore. I was too exhausted.

At that moment, I decided I would hang up my cleats. It was time to retire. When it came to it, the decision was very easy. My body couldn't handle the pressure of the sport anymore. I couldn't handle the physical stress that football put on me, and I had certainly had enough of the mental stress. My blood pressure skyrocketed on a regular basis. I had to provide for my family, yes, but first and foremost, I had to be there for my family.

I had played sports since I was seven years old. I had fought for years to make it to the NFL. I achieved that goal, and I am proud of myself. I fought tooth and nail every day just to make it in. I even became a starter in my first year after being undrafted. I beat the odds. Now I was 25 years old and fighting for my life. I would have to put the same effort into that. I needed to be there for my son.

The NFL has its ups and downs. It was fun playing in the league, and I learned a lot. I was able to do things most people only dream of doing. I was able to party with people whom I never would have been able to meet had I not played in the league. I made decent money. It didn't equal out to what I had to put my body through on a weekly basis, but it was more than I could have imagined making fresh out of college. But none of the money, partying, or vacations can compete with the people I met. I came into contact with thousands of fans who showed me love and respect. I made connections with businesspeople who will always have their doors open for me. I always networked while I was in the NFL, because I knew it wouldn't last forever. In the end, I used the NFL because I knew it was using me.

My body went through a beating every day in the league. I was once told that every time you take a big hit in the NFL, it is equivalent to being in a car accident. Mondays after games were rough. It was a battle just to get out of bed. My body felt like it was 50 years old. My back hurt, my muscles ached, and my joints were tight and cracked every time I moved. I often felt like the Tin Man from "The Wizard of Oz," needing someone to put a little oil here and there just to get me going. And that was just the normal wear and tear of an NFL season. The injuries were a totally different story. Everyone gets injured during the course of a season. You just have to be able to play through the pain. We didn't have much time to recover after games, because we were expected to be fully ready for practice every Wednesday. Playing hurt was more about the fear of losing your spot than about doing it for the team.

The concussions were the scariest part of the job. We all felt the short-term effects and were terrified to consider the long-term effects. When Junior Seau committed suicide in 2012 because of his struggle with brain damage, it changed the sport. He was a legend in the game, and I believe his last act in life will make him even more legendary. Seau ended his life with a shot to the chest because he wanted his brain, and the trauma it had suffered, to be studied.

One of the biggest problems with retiring was the reaction of my family and friends. When I first made it to the NFL, hands were out. Everybody needed something. Everybody felt as if they were entitled to some money because we had the same genes. The people closest to me were the worst. They acted as if we had gone through this journey together. Sure, they were there on game days or sent their texts, but where were they on hospital days? They just liked knowing someone famous.

A lot of people said that I had changed, like I thought I was better than everyone else because I had made it. The truth is that I did change, but they didn't. I balanced staying true to myself with understanding that I was now a different person. I no longer had any desire to do the things everyone back home was still doing. Partying, hanging on the streets, and chasing women was child's play. But I was the same Donald Jones, the humble person who held onto his roots and learned how to be a better man while away.

Pretty much every time I went out with family and friends, I was expected to pick up the tab. If the bill came and I didn't immediately grab it, there were always a few who threw me insulted looks. People would flat-out ask me for money, coming up with the craziest of reasons. My family tree sprouted new branches, and I had people calling themselves my cousins who looked somewhat familiar, but whose names didn't register. I had family members concoct outrageous lies to get money. Lots of people asked me to invest in their ideas or go into business with them. I began screening my calls, because telling people "no" just made them try harder.

I thought I had put that problem to bed, but when I got firmer about not giving handouts, people started talking about me behind my back. They talked about what they had heard I did with my money and whom I was spending it on. I have always been family-oriented, so I refused to miss family functions because of this nonsense, but that typically meant that I would sit in a room full of relatives and feel totally alone. Eventually, I began to distance myself from my family and friends because I was tired of all the negativity. When I was still playing in the NFL, during breaks I would go on vacation instead of home. My teammates became my family. They understood exactly what I was going through. We shared stories of how uncles we had looked up to our whole lives would lie straight to our faces to get money. My teammates were the ones I spent holidays and partied with. We became known as the "Bills' Mafia," and many of us chose to spend more time with our fans than our families, because we knew how to appreciate and enjoy the moment. Nothing else mattered.

Playing in the NFL eliminates any privacy you might want. Every time you step out of your home, you are under scrutiny. Everything you do is magnified. Every time you walk into a store, people know who you are. They want autographs and pictures. You have to be nice, because it's part of your job. It comes with the fame. The fans pay your bills, so you have to be all smiles even when you are having a rough day. I would walk into places with my family, and they would want to let people know who I was. They were proud relatives, but they couldn't understand my craving for normalcy. They loved the attention my career brought. I hated it.

Chapter Nine

The "N" Word

I retired from the NFL because the sport was too dangerous for my health. My kidneys were working at less than 20 percent of their normal capacity. My creatinine level was seven times higher than my doctors wanted it to be. Despite my career being over and my confidence shaken, I still worked out every day. I did my best to live a normal life. The toughest part was hearing people say, "But you look so healthy." That led me to doubt my doctors, because I also thought I looked healthy, and most of the time I felt perfectly fine.

The doctors told me I was able to do the things I did because of how physically fit I was. My six-foot frame had a lot of muscle mass, so my body could withstand more than most. But now, I had to fully change my diet. I had to stay away from sodium because of my blood pressure. I had to avoid potassium, too, which was very hard. I didn't realize how many foods contained high levels of potassium, including the foods I thought were healthiest. The potassium molecule is bigger than most. That means it moves through the filter of the kidneys slower, and it's hard for someone with damaged kidneys to process it.

Ignorance may be bliss, but if I was going to face this head on, I needed to know the facts. I reached out to organizations like the National Kidney Foundation and the NephCure Foundation. The IgA Foundation of America actually reached out to me. I needed to be a part of those organizations because it helped to meet people going through the same struggle.

The first few people I met with IgA nephropathy, also called Berger's disease, looked as if they were on their deathbeds. Their bodies were in a state of atrophy. Their eyes were swollen, as if they had been punched in the face several times. They vomited constantly. They gained weight because of the steroids they were taking. They had no energy. It made me wonder: *How close am I to that stage of my sickness? How close am I to death?* Obviously, I didn't want to get to that point. I didn't want to be sick all the time. The dialysis machine became the demon in my dreams. I broke into a sweat when I found myself in the same room with the monster. I had heard so many dreadful stories about it, but I had also heard it wasn't that bad. I was hoping never to find out the truth.

I still couldn't understand why this had happened to me. But then I sat back and looked at things from a distance. That was when I came to the conclusion that I needed to be the person to beat this disease and teach the world. I had to be an example for everyone dealing with health issues or personal issues that they could pull through anything with the right attitude. Mind over matter, right? It was time for me to get healthy so I could achieve my new purpose and stop focusing only on myself. The football chapter of my life was over, and I was ready to start writing the next one. I stayed very positive. I knew if my mind went negative, my body would follow.

In September 2013, the doctors told me I wouldn't make it past Christmas without a transplant or dialysis. I told them I wanted to start looking for a new kidney immediately. I started informing everyone in my family of the procedure and how to get tested to see if they were a blood match. Multiple family members volunteered. I was wary at first about asking, because I didn't know what their motives might be. There were times when a family member offered their organ and my first thought was, "Why would I want it from you?" I shouldn't have thought that way.

Luckily, my father stepped up and told me that he wanted to be the first to get tested. We sat and talked about how it would be a sign from above if we were a match. My father brought me into this world, and now he would possibly give me a second life. I sat back and thought about the time he had called me after watching the movie *John Q*, in which Denzel Washington's character went through a similar situation to the one my dad was going through now. After my father saw the movie, he called me and said, "Just know that I would do the same for you." The two of us could never have imagined that we would find ourselves in a similar boat. We just needed to make our own fairy-tale ending.

My dad was very excited to get his test done. I am blood type O+, which is the most common type. My dad could be O+ or O- and still be a match. That would only be the first hurdle, though. He would have to take several health tests; like father, like son. In order to give me his kidney, my dad would have to pass his blood and urine tests with flying colors. He could have no trace of kidney disease, high blood pressure, or diabetes. In black communities, it is almost unheard of for a man his age to show no signs of those conditions, which frightened us. Also, my dad never went to the doctor for physicals or check-ups because he was always working, and in his mind, that was the best way to stay healthy. It was around this point that we realized the odds were not exactly in our favor.

We each went through a series of tests. The first time we went to the doctor together, I had to see five specialists: a transplant nephrologist, surgeon, transplant coordinator, social worker, and psychologist. They had to make sure I was mentally, physically, and financially stable enough to have a transplant. Finances were a big part of the equation, as the medications I would have to take after the surgery are expensive. They took vial after vial of blood from me that day. After the fifth vial, I started to wonder if this was really happening. After the 10th vial, I wondered if they were going to leave me with any blood. After what was about the 30th vial, with my head spinning and my ability to add fading, I could only look up to God. We were at New York Presbyterian Hospital all day. They tested every inch of my body. They tested me for every disease known to man. I remember my father glancing my way with a look suggesting that he was wondering what he had really signed up for. He hated needles. Previously, we had gone to get flu shots and he had cringed as if the needle were a dagger. I started to wonder if I had asked too much of him.

My dad's first test was to see if he was a match. If so, that would open the door for a slew of tests of his health. He had his own team of doctors that was entirely separate from mine. That was so there would be no conflict of interest. His doctors would look after him to make sure that he was healthy and that surgery would present no major risks to him. My doctors would look after me. They would take care of us during the pre-surgery process, during surgery, and after surgery.

He took the test for his blood type, and we waited. The doctors said it would be a week before the results came back. It was the longest week of my life. I prayed every day that he was a match. The week went by and we didn't hear from the doctors. I started to worry. So did my dad. He called me multiple times to ask why it was taking so long. I had no answer for him, or for the rest of my family.

I was at the grocery store when I finally received the call. I recognized the number right away, and my heart dropped. I wanted my dad to be a match so badly. I was terrified that they would tell me he wasn't. One of my parents had to be a match, but my mom had a history of high blood pressure, so she wouldn't be able to donate even if she was. I prayed, and my prayers were answered.

That news lifted the world from my shoulders, even though the doctor told me, "Don't get too excited yet, because he still has to be in full health." I called my father and told him as soon as I hung up with the doctors. I could tell he was excited by the way he responded. It sounded like he wanted to cry. I called my mom and gave her the great news, as well.

My father went through more tests than I did. During one visit to the hospital, the phlebotomist took 25 vials of blood from him. He began to get discouraged. Between tests, he joked with me and said things like, "You better know I love you." We talked about how many people backed out amid the testing process for donating an organ, but we both understood that these tests were necessary.

After I had sat alone with my dad for an hour of philosophical ramblings, the doctors came back and informed him that he was fully healthy and could be my donor. They told us we could set a date for the surgery. We had two options: December 17, 2013, which was my birthday, or December 3. I chose December 3 because I wanted to be back home for my birthday and Christmas, not in a hospital bed. More importantly, I felt I had to pick the earliest date possible so as not to draw out this ordeal for my dad.

Everything was going smoothly as we counted down the days until the surgery, but then we hit a snag. The doctors found a small cyst on my father's kidney. The day my father called me with that news, I cried. Everything to do with the transplant had fallen into place when I needed it to, and now we might be denied this opportunity when our hopes were so high. We were only about a week away from the surgery. The doctors put him on steroids for one day to try to get the cyst to go down. They told him if it didn't, he could still be my donor, but they would have to remove the cyst during the transplant surgery.

I was blessed to have my father as my donor. People die every day on transplant waiting lists, but I had somebody who was willing and able to give me a kidney. It was fate.

I once believed that all parents would donate an organ for their child if faced with the decision. However, during this experience, I ran into several people who had needed organs and whose parents wouldn't give them one. One woman told me she had asked her dad to donate a kidney to her. His response was, "What about my other kids?" What type of person says that to his child? She said she felt abandoned and hadn't spoken to him since. This whole process gave me a new perspective on family.

As the day drew nearer, my father became more and more nervous. He asked a lot of questions that I couldn't answer. He became so nervous that his blood pressure went up. He had never had high blood pressure before. The doctors told him that if his pressure didn't go down, they would have no choice but to postpone the surgery. I kept trying to tell him that everything was going to be all right and that this was a common surgery. I had already come to terms with the fact that it was all in God's hands. If something went wrong, then it was meant to happen. On a daily basis, I reminded my father of Reinhold Niebuhr's famous quote: "God, grant me the serenity to accept the things that I cannot change, the courage to change the things that I can, and the wisdom to know the difference." It was difficult to get my father to see it that way. He had so many questions and doubts. I just wanted the procedure done so I could move on with my life. I was tired of being sick and tired. I was tired of feeling cold from anemia. I wanted to eat regular meals. I just wanted to feel normal again.

On December 3, I woke up after only an hour of sleep. It was finally the day of surgery. It turned out I had been so focused on the surgery itself and on my dad's well-being that I hadn't packed a thing for what was underestimated to be three or four days in the hospital, so I had to scramble to pack and get everything ready. I had to be at my father's house at 4 a.m., because we needed to be at the hospital by 5:30. I rushed over, and he had two pastors there waiting to say a prayer. He had a fire burning in the back yard. We gathered around the fire and prayed. The prayer was so beautiful, it brought tears to everyone's eyes. The anticipation was growing minute by minute. After the prayer, we rushed to my truck, and my uncle took the wheel.

The ride to New York Presbyterian Hospital was surreal. I stared out the window into the dark night skies as we merged onto the New Jersey Turnpike. Everyone in the truck was quiet; their nerves were at an all-time high. I was surprised to find that I wasn't nervous. "Excited" summed up my mood. I knew we would be okay, because I had prayed on it and accepted that God has a plan. As we got closer to the hospital, though, my nerves finally started to shake. We got to the George Washington Bridge, and I could see the hospital building. I looked out at the water as we crossed the bridge. The moon shone over the serene Hudson River. I glanced at the New York City skyline, focusing on the recently finished Freedom Tower, and thought about the act of reconstructing one's life.

We pulled up in front of the hospital, which was eerily quiet. I checked in at the front desk. "I'm here for surgery," I whispered to the security guard at the front desk. "Go around the corner to the elevators to the fourth floor," he said without looking my way.

We got to the fourth floor and checked in. Everyone who was having surgery that morning arrived around the same time. My mom and the rest of the family got there 30 minutes later. Nervousness permeated the room, and strangers tried to offer one another comforting looks. We sat and talked about everything that was going to happen. Most of my family seemed anxious, so I recommended that they get something to eat. I was very hungry, having had to fast before the surgery, and I hoped desperately that one of them would grab me a little something. That thought faded quickly when I remembered the doctor telling me that he regularly sent people home because they thought they could get away with sneaking a bite, and their systems weren't empty for surgery.

It took the medical team some time to get ready for the many surgeries they had that day. We sat in the waiting area and watched the clock. The nurses came out and began calling people back to get prepped. They called me next to last, by which point I was a bit of a wreck. I hugged everybody and took the long walk back.

The overly polite nurses directed me into the prep area, which had an emergency-room feeling. They told me to remove all my clothes and put on the hospital gown; that would be my last smile of the day. They stepped out of the room while I changed, then let my family come back to speak with me for a little longer. I kept thinking about my father in a room down the hall. After lying in bed for 30 minutes, my curiosity got the best of me, so I got up and walked across the floor to make sure my father was okay, all the while holding the back of my gown as best as I could so as not to give anyone a free show.

He was very quiet, almost meditative, as he waited on the doctors. I told him once more that he would be okay. Then I went back to my room and got in bed. The nurses came back to tell me what I should expect. My family sat with me for an hour, waiting for the word. Then the doctors came out and told me that my father's surgery had already begun. They brought the anesthesiologist out to meet me. He explained his job while inserting the IV that would stay in my arm until I left the hospital. The doctor said that it would be another hour before they called me, because they had to finish my father's surgery before they did mine. A nurse offered me a remote control to the television, but I found the small talk with my relatives to be more soothing.

In the weeks before the surgery, I had envisioned my dad and I being in the room together, side by side. I thought that he would have his own team of doctors working on him, and that they would take the kidney out of him and put it straight into me. It's funny the things that go through your mind, relying on Hollywood's portrayal of things when you really have no clue what's going to happen.

An hour went by, and the nurses finally came to get me. I didn't expect to walk into the operating room myself, but that's exactly what happened. They walked me back and explained to me everything that was going to happen. The lights were blinding; it reminded me of when I had stepped onto the field for my first NFL game and couldn't see much because the lights blurred my vision. The doctors and nurses all had masks on, so I couldn't really tell who was who. I was asked to disrobe. The only thing I could think of at that moment was that I had no control over what was about to happen. The nurses laid me on the cold operating table. I looked around at everything in the room. The anesthesiologist walked in and made sure I was ready. He started talking to me about football as he administered the anesthesia through my IV. I felt it tingle in my veins. He told me he was a New York Giants fan. Before I could tell him that I had grown up a Giants fan, I was asleep.

I was put under around 8:30 a.m. and awoke at 7 p.m. I was in a lot of discomfort when I opened my eyes; everything was either numb or sore. I looked down and I saw that I had over 30 staples in my stomach. I was amazed looking at them. It looked like I had a zipper coming up the middle of my stomach, and if I wanted to check out their handiwork, I could just unzip. I also realized I had a catheter coming out of me. It was very uncomfortable. My family stood over me. I said a few words to reassure them, but I don't think I made sense, because I was still drowsy from the anesthesia. The main sensation I felt was the need to urinate. I asked if I could get up, but the nurses told me no. They said that it was normal for me to feel that way after surgery, but that I didn't really have to go. I insisted, so they gave me a bedpan. I couldn't sit up, so they had to lay it underneath me. The nurses were right; I couldn't go. So I closed my eyes and fell right back to sleep lying on the bedpan. I woke up a couple of hours later and added back pain to my list of aches.

I was in and out of sleep for a couple of hours in the recovery room before they took me up to the place where I would recuperate. My nurse was very nice. She managed to get me my own private room, which I loved. She also positioned me so I could have a bird's-eye view of New York City. Having my own room relaxed me and made me feel more comfortable, which was good, because I was going to be in the hospital a lot longer than I or the doctors had anticipated.

My first night in the hospital went well. The annoying part was that they had to keep coming into my room to take vitals and draw blood every 15 minutes. They also had to administer my meds. Every single time they came in to give me drugs, they explained what each one was and what it did. It was protocol, but I just wanted to sleep. I took nine medications in the form of 16 pills. I took tacrolimus and Myfortic twice a day to prevent organ rejection. I will be on those two medications for the rest of my life in order to fight nephropathy, or the "N" word, as I now call it; perhaps not calling it by its name will take away some of its power. I took labetalol and valsartan for my blood pressure. It was possible I would be on those for the rest of my life, as well, depending on whether my blood pressure leveled out. The rest of the meds I would gradually stop taking as time went on. They included Valcyte, Sulfam, and Zantac. I felt so toxic taking all of those pills twice a day. They also put me on prednisone again. Every time I went to sleep, they came in and woke me up. I kept thinking: *I am 25 years old, stuck in a hospital bed, forced to take all these meds. I should still be playing football and enjoying life.*

I had to get used to maneuvering with the IV and catheter. Every hour, I felt like I had to go to the bathroom, but I couldn't. Every time, I would get out of bed and walk to the bathroom. The catheter was attached to a pouch, which was connected by a clear tube. The tube would get caught on the side of the bed. I would move so fast from an urge to use the bathroom that I would forget about it. The catheter also gave me sharp, contraction-like pains, which ran through my groin to the point where I couldn't move. I would tense up for about 10 seconds, and then the pain would go away.

The doctors kept me on a strict liquid diet. The only things I could eat were Jell-O, flavored ices, and apple juice. A nutritionist came and informed me of what I could and could not eat moving forward. The two main things I couldn't have were grapefruits and pomegranate, because they would counteract my anti-rejection medications. The fact that they somehow managed to pick my two favorite fruits got me thinking a conspiracy was taking place. Either way, I would have to get used to these and many more lifestyle changes if I wanted to keep this kidney for a long time, because my body could reject it at any point down the road. Then I would have to get a new one and go through this entire ordeal again, and maybe next time I wouldn't be so lucky as to skip the waiting list and dialysis.

The next day, I was up and walking around. I walked to my father's room down the hall to check on him. He was in a little bit of pain, but he was doing well. The doctors and nurses encouraged us both to stand up and walk. They wanted us to move around so we could get our bowels working again. My father's system started working fast, and he was able to leave two days after the surgery. My bowels, however, appeared to be on strike. I guess I have to make everything in my life complicated to make for a better story.

My second night in the hospital was very different from the first. A pain came over me that I had never felt before. I squirmed in my bed for hours. I asked the nurses for more and more pain meds. They would come in and insert the drugs through my IV — *the juices tickling my veins with their magic fingertips.* My eyes would roll around in my head because it felt so good. I would fall asleep while they were still administering the drugs. But 15 minutes later, I would wake up in more pain. The nurses and doctors told me that my bowels would be the last part of my body to start working again after the anesthesia. They thought that was the problem, but it wasn't.

The discomfort felt like bad gas pains, and it wouldn't quit. The nurses insisted I walk, but I didn't have the energy, and I was in too much pain. Every time I got up, I would get into the main hallway and feel like I was going to pass out. I also had to pull around this cart with my monitor and a bag full of urine. I would lean on the pole of the cart as I struggled to summon the energy to walk.

I would go lie back down, but that didn't help either. I couldn't get comfortable. I tried every position, lying in bed and sitting in a chair, to see if it would ease the pain, but nothing worked. On top of that, I kept having these sharp pains in my penis and bladder. I needed the doctors to find out what was wrong with me so that my mind could stop conjuring up worst-case scenarios. I begged every nurse who came into the room for more and more pain meds. They were only allowed to administer the drugs every four hours. With the pain relief from each dose lasting 15 to 20 minutes, that was not going to work for me. I felt helpless. My family sat and looked at me. They kept saying they wished they could do something. I wished they could, too.

The doctors ran various tests. They did a biopsy to make sure I wasn't rejecting the kidney. They also wanted to see if the disease had come back, as it was known to recur. This biopsy was a lot easier than previous ones because my kidney was positioned in the front, right next to my stomach. I hardly felt the needle. My stomach was still numb from the surgical incision and the staples. Even if it had hurt, I wouldn't have had the energy to fight them.

I received bittersweet results from the biopsy. The good news was that I didn't have any signs of rejection or of the disease recurring. But the biopsy did show why I was in so much pain. The doctors told me I had a leak between my bladder and my kidney. Urine was leaking into my stomach. They said they would have to do an emergency surgery and insert a stent. I didn't care what they did at that point. I just needed the pain to stop.

I went through the second surgery in the middle of the night, after we received the biopsy results. I felt a lot better when I woke up in the recovery room this time. I still had the catheter, but now I also had a tube coming from my side, draining fluids. Every time I moved, I had to carry the tube. Sometimes I forgot it was there, and I would get up and it would yank my side, as if the bed were reaching out to pull me back into its grasp. The nurses came into my room every couple of hours to drain that tube as it filled with blood.

After a few hours of no pain, it suddenly returned. They ran more tests, which showed that my stomach was backed up. It felt like I had swallowed way too much air. My stomach felt like a balloon that was slowly inflating. The doctors told me that it looked like a balloon on my X-ray. When they pressed on my stomach, it was hard. Nothing wanted to give. They had to get my bowels to begin working again, because they were preventing my system from running its course.

They gave me laxatives multiple times a day. I drank prune juice. They gave me everything they could to get me to go to the bathroom. Nothing worked. At this point, I was willing to do anything to make the pain stop. I didn't have the energy to fight anymore. The doctors came in and told me they had to put a tube down my nose. I thought they were joking in an attempt to relax my muscles so I could have a bowel movement. They weren't. This tube would go in through my nose, down my throat, and into my stomach. They said it would pump the fluids out.

The first time they tried to insert the tube, it didn't work. They had to put it in while I was awake because I had to swallow it into my stomach. They gave me water while they did the procedure to help me swallow, but they couldn't get the tube past my throat. They inserted with a bit of pressure, which made me gag and vomit. My nose began pouring blood. I begged them to stop. They had to figure something else out. They said the only other thing they could give me was laxatives. With a tube going in one nostril and blood squirting out the other, I agreed and prayed that they would work.

I was in pain for another day before the doctors came back and told me they had to try the tube again. I shouted "No!" in a knee-jerk response, then felt embarrassed. I kept flashing back to when they had tried to do it the first time and blood had erupted out of my nose. After much pleading from my family, I finally agreed. The doctors said they would try a smaller tube that should go down a little easier. They said the only problem was that the smaller tubes had been known to clog during the process of draining the fluids. Every ounce of me was against going through that process again, but I needed to ease this pain. Plus, it was the only option left on the table.

Since it was my family who had talked me into giving it another go, I put them to work. My mom held a pan in case I had to throw up, which was sure to happen. My aunt held the cup of water that I had to drink as I was swallowing the tube to help it go down smoothly. My grandmother held my hand and prayed with me. My other aunt got up and walked out of the room after I started assigning duties. She and I joke about it to this day, and I still call her a punk for not being able to handle watching me go through the procedure she had begged me to undergo.

The doctors began to insert the tube through my nose, and I began to drink the water. Most times, I gagged and everything came right back up. The doctors stopped and let me vomit, but they didn't pull the tube out. They started up again when I was finished, pushing the tube gradually farther and farther until they got it all the way down and it began draining green fluids out of my stomach. And just like that, the pain started easing. I could see my stomach slowly lowering. I couldn't help but watch the fluids flow into the big jar behind my bed and think: On a normal day, when someone passes gas, it creates an awkward situation, but when someone's health is on the line and everyone is pulling for him, a jar full of waste and the occasional squeak from below are seen as gifts from God.

The procedure was going well until the tube clogged. The doctors told me they would have to take it out and go with the bigger size after all, which was what I had feared. They pulled out the small tube, which rubbed against my organs, and started the process all over.

The doctors managed to get the bigger tube in, and it started working. It pumped a liter and a half of green fluid from my stomach, which was bizarre because I couldn't remember eating anything green that day. The amount of fluid that I had in my stomach was amazing. The pain finally stopped, but I still had this tube down my nose. The doctors told me I had to keep it in for 24 hours. I had still had no bowel movements, and they didn't want the fluid to build back up. I now had three tubes draining my body from three different places. A few months earlier, I had been preparing for a football season, and now I was lying here feeling like a science experiment.

As the night went on, I told my mom I didn't think I could last 24 hours like that. She said I would be fine. I did the best I could. I fell asleep with the tube in. But after six hours, I couldn't take it anymore. I couldn't sleep because I couldn't get comfortable. I kept waking up and changing positions. I could feel the tube sitting in the back of my throat. Finally, in the middle of the night, I warned my mother that I was taking it out. I couldn't go another minute with this thing in me. She begged me not to, but the anxiety took over, and I felt a panic attack coming on. I did the one thing my doctors had made me promise I wouldn't do. I pulled the tube out. The look on my mother's face as I took it out was one of hysterics. The doctors came into the room, and they were fuming mad. They said the pain would come back, and they would have to put the tube back in and go through everything again from the start. I didn't care. I said if we had to put it back in, so be it. But then, about 20 minutes later, the craziest moment of my life happened. I had my first bowel movement since the surgery, and it was all up from there. It was beyond stupid and risky for me to take matters in my own hands when things weren't working, but I got lucky, or perhaps I was Dr. Jones in a previous life.

After my first bowel movement, I had a small problem. The doctors had been giving me laxatives for a couple of days, so I had to go to the bathroom constantly, and things got ugly. It was difficult to control myself. I'll spare you most of the details and just say that my family had to keep changing the bed sheets. I didn't care at that point, as I was so weak from fighting all of the pain. Everybody who was in the hospital saw every part of my body, but I didn't care. I was just thrilled that the pain was finally gone and that the toughest part of the procedure was done.

The next day, the doctors upgraded my diet. They told me that my appetite would come back slowly and that I shouldn't rush it. But I wanted to eat a real meal so badly. It had been well over a week since I'd had one. I asked a volunteer at the hospital to get me something to eat from the cafeteria. I told her I would pay her if she went and got me something. She told me she would get me whatever I wanted, and she didn't want any money. She simply did it out of the kindness of her heart. I would later find out that she had given an organ to her daughter years before. It was amazing how nice she was to me, and that there really are people out there like her. I only saw her that day and after she brought me a meal, never again. She was like a guardian angel in the hospital.

My mouth watered as I prepared to eat, but I took one bite and felt full. I also felt as if I was going to vomit. I guess that was what the doctors meant when they said to take it slow. I pushed the meal over to the side. Every now and then I tried another bite, but that was all I could handle.

My last day in the hospital couldn't come fast enough. I was so excited to be going home. I was ready to start a new chapter in my life. I would have to get used to a lifestyle with limits, but I had learned from sports how to adjust to new situations.

My life has forever changed because of my kidney disease. I will always be on medications to keep my body from rejecting my father's kidney. I take 16 pills twice a day, and I do it with a smile on my face because I am just happy to be alive. Those pills suppress my immune system, so I always have to be careful around people who might be sick. That means I have to wear a mask in public. I never really paid much attention to people around me coughing, sneezing, or spreading germs. Now I feel like the germs are attacking me whenever I hear them cough or sneeze. People stare at me as if I am from a different planet and might transmit something to them. It's a big adjustment at my age to get used to people staring at me like this, but I have gotten used to it. It's something that I have to deal with for the rest of my life.

At 25, I should be having fun. I should still be playing in the NFL, partying with my friends. I could complain about my life, but that won't get me anywhere. Complaining is not going to help others. Complaining is not going to feed my family. We all complain about things, but there are always millions out there who have it worse. I could have died waiting on a transplant list. I was always taught that every day above ground is a good day. One of my best friends once said to me, "It's bigger than football for you." He never talked like that. He was always joking like the big kid he was. When he said that to me, it really hit home. I often ask myself, *why am I going through this? Why did this happen to me in the prime of my life, right when I was about to sign a major contract?* But then I sit back and say, *why not me?* I am still alive for a reason. Maybe I am supposed to be the one to wake up the world; I am sure we can all agree that it needs a reality check. Maybe I am supposed to help others like me. Sometimes you have to take yourself out of the equation. For a moment, place your focus on others, and a distorted picture can become HD.

When I was younger, I woke up every day and my mission was to be a professional football player. I accomplished that mission. Now, when I wake up every day, my mission is to take over the world like the characters in the famous cartoon *Pinky and The Brain*. I want to create things that change the world.

Chapter Ten

Set the World on Fire

What really solidified my decision to retire was when the Colts tried to recruit me after the Patriots released me. The Colts were big on me. It was well documented that their head coach, Chuck Pagano, had issues with his health. The team's general manager was the first to call me. He told me that they didn't want to sign me just to have another body in camp, but that they really wanted me to play. The GM then had Coach Pagano call me. We talked for an hour about what it was like to deal with serious health problems. He talked about how well I would fit in with the team and how much they wanted me. It made me feel great, because they were serious playoff contenders most years. I wanted to be a part of that.

They were the first team ever to make me do a stress test. In my opinion, it was God's work. If it hadn't been for the stress test, I wouldn't have known that my blood pressure could spike off the charts.

After the test, I left the hospital and went back to the stadium to meet the coaches. I ate lunch with the team. Everyone tried to sell me on the organization as I walked through the building. They told me it was a family atmosphere, which I desired after my brief stint in New England. I spent an hour talking to Coach Pagano and the rest of the coaches in the lunchroom.

Then everything went south. They started to act funny. I could tell that they had gotten the bad news back from the doctors. I went into the general manager's office, and he told me they had decided to sign someone else. I knew what had really happened, but there was nothing I could do. I thanked him as I walked out of his office to head back to the airport. It didn't even hurt that badly, because I knew at that point that I was retiring. I called home and told everyone what had happened and that I was tired of the business. I was done playing. My mind had been unsettled ever since my short run in New England, so it was a relief. It was time for me to move on to the next chapter and live.

Does it surprise you that the NFL works closely with the FBI when it comes to background checks on potential players? Or, to put it another way, does it come as any surprise that the billionaire owners of NFL teams have connections within the FBI who do background checks before the owners invest millions of dollars in a 21-year-old straight out of college? Once the players are cleared and signed, they are used not only for their skills, but also as character references for future players. And I can't lie — when it came to a majority of the college players I was asked about, let's just say the teams had good reason to be inquiring.

When I visit public schools these days to chat with at-risk students, I get many unfiltered questions from them — the top three being: "Are you a millionaire?" "What's it like seeing yourself on the Madden football game?" and "What was your first major purchase once you made it to the NFL?" None of their questions bother me, because at that age, meeting a professional sports player makes that fantasy world on television seem a bit more real. Another question I inevitably get is how much money I made playing in the NFL. I answer that I was paid the minimum annual salary of $420,000, mostly because I was a walk-on and not drafted.

Most students think I am crazy when I argue that $420,000 is really not a lot of money when you consider that the average NFL player's career is only three and a half seasons — not to mention when you consider what you put your body through to earn it. You can potentially shave years off your life expectancy by playing in the NFL, taking hits that lead to concussions or becoming one of the many former professional athletes addicted to painkillers. A player has to pay his agent 3 percent of his contract before taxes. NFL players have to pay taxes in every state that they have a game in. I paid taxes in nine states every year. My agents received 15 to 20 percent of all off-the-field endorsements they brought to me. I had other expenses, too, that drastically subtracted from that original $420,000. Once I got into the NFL, I saw how many players were actually "thousandaires" instead of millionaires. Unfortunately, the public is blinded by the sensational, record-breaking contracts shown on ESPN. Their knee-jerk response is to say how overpaid athletes are, and we all get painted over with the same wide brushstroke. Just once, I would like to hear a fan say that the billionaire owners, who aren't putting their bodies at risk every day, are the ones who are overpaid, but I don't see that day coming anytime soon. The fact is, that's the way the world works. The owners have the money to control the team, so they just sit back and collect their checks.

During school visits, I lay out my three ground rules: Don't try to get me to make negative comments about any celebrities, keep the questions and comments G- and PG-rated, and since you get to ask me questions, it's only fair that I get to ask a few in return. With those guidelines set, when their questions begin to turn silly or slow down, I take out my lucky half dollar and offer them my "By the Way" or "BTW" (I try to speak their language whenever I can) History Challenge. Holding the coin in the air, I ask the students, "Anyone ever take part in the BTW Challenge?" I always get blank looks. "Okay, then, who's up for taking the BTW Challenge right now?" Most hands shoot straight up; the rest rise hesitantly. "Okay," I say, "the BTW Challenge is simple. I am going to give you a bunch of clues about a famous person, and you will try to figure out who it is." Most are eager to play, because anything is better than my leaving and them returning to their textbooks. "So, let's start! Who was the very first African-American to be featured on a U.S. coin? The one I am currently holding in my hand." All eyes are on the coin for a clue. "BTW, the first person who gives me the correct first and last name, after raising his or her hand and being called on by me, will get to keep my lucky coin. Oh, each person can only make one guess, so it might be beneficial to hear all six clues." To make it more tempting, I add, "BTW, this coin sells for anywhere between $25 and $500, depending on its condition." And that is the moment when all the students are hooked.

After they shoot out a few incorrect guesses and I ask for one thing the class knows about each person mentioned, I keep offering clues until someone guesses correctly, we run out of clues, or everybody has taken their one guess. "BTW, this person was also the first African-American to be featured on a U.S. stamp." "BTW, this person was born a slave and wrote a famous book titled *Up from Slavery*." "BTW, this person had an African-American mother and a white father." "BTW, this person was the first African-American to be invited to the White House. He was invited by

Theodore Roosevelt, our 26th U.S. president." "BTW, this person established the Tuskegee Institute, the only university in our country whose campus is designated as a National Historic Site." At this point, a great deal of good guesses have been given and many interesting facts about those people discussed by the class, but rarely do they come up with the correct answer. At that point, I put my lucky half dollar in my pocket and declare the challenge to be over. The students ask for a second guess each, but I remind them that rules are rules and we had a deal. When they ask for the answer, I respond, "BTW." They give me confused looks, so I slow down and speak softer: "The answer is B.T.W." I pause for a moment, and that's when a few light bulbs go off, and a couple students, around the same time, excitedly shout out the answer: "Booker T. Washington." And I smile at the beautiful educational moment just created.

Oh, any guesses as to their next question? That would be, "Mr. Jones, do you have any more lucky coins in your pocket?" And we all have a great, memorable laugh.

The only place that comes close to being on an NFL field for me is a classroom. Both places have so much energy and excitement, and when I can't just walk to an NFL stadium, the place I go to feel most alive is a public school classroom. Now, I know my half hour or so with students doesn't offer me the everyday feel or reality of classroom life, which can be tedious and unruly at times. But I know a few good teachers whose rooms are as high-paced every day as they are when I am there.

When I leave the school and walk out to my car, things really start to sink in. Those kids were excited about learning. I went to a school where most students receive free or reduced-price lunches, and they were thirsty for the answer to my History Challenge. They asked me to elaborate on my key philosophies, both on sports and on life. True, there was a monetary reward to the History Challenge, but I reached them. A guy who never took a single education class in college, and didn't know any of the students' names or past behaviors before he entered that room, went in there and taught them several things they'll remember for a long time — like the difference between obedience and respect, why I believe "anticipation" is the most important word in sports and life, and that a closed mouth doesn't get fed.

Shortly after I retired, I scheduled a business meeting at the Viacom Building in New York City with Tom Calderone, the president of VH1. We had become friends, and I wanted to pitch him an idea for a show in order to get some things going before my surgery. He invited two executives who produced the show "Love & Hip Hop." It was a scorcher of a day, and despite being dressed in my best three-piece suit, I decided to take the train into the city to soak up the Manhattan vibe. During the ride over, I started to feel a bit woozy; I hoped that it was only because I had skipped breakfast. I had planned to get there early enough to eat in the city before the meeting. Right after getting some food into my system, I met up with my partner, Claudia Ruffin, and we went over the finer points of our plan right up until we walked into Calderone's office.

The meeting started off with casual introductions, and then it was time for me to get on the mound and pitch away. As I started to speak, I realized how powerful the people in the room were, and I became nervous and sweaty. After a minute or two, I could feel my body temperature rising, and that was when the dizziness came over me. I had no choice but to ignore Claudia's reassuring look, urging me to work through it, and ask if I could excuse myself for a moment to use the bathroom. Somewhere in the hallway, the lights went out. I passed out and apparently hit my mouth on a table. As I was regaining consciousness, I realized that I had no shirt on and that the two producers were standing over me waving clipboards, trying to cool me off. Once I realized what had just happened, I tried to break the tension: "I hope I didn't mess up the interview." They had a good laugh and told me, "Of course not," but I knew I had fumbled.

They called the paramedics to make sure it wasn't something serious. Once I was given the thumbs-up, I apologized and thanked everyone again. I called my doctor after we left the building, and he told me that my blood pressure had dropped because of the medications I was on. He said he would change my prescriptions so it wouldn't happen again. I couldn't believe that at 25, I was still going through these episodes.

Kiion means everything to me. He brings me joy every day. He is such a happy child. There is no better feeling than when your child's eyes light up when he sees you come home. Every time my son spots me, he runs to me screaming, "Daddy!" Every time I walk in the house, he lights up like a Christmas tree, which we can now afford. I have worked hard my entire life in order to be able to have something as small as a Christmas tree with gifts under it. I have to work twice as hard now, because I am in a world, which is unknown to me. Writing speeches, books, or starting a business from the ground up can be very stressful. It's even harder when you have been playing sports your entire life and dedicated every second to it. My son is always there to pick me up. I can be having the worst day, and he will brighten me up with the simplest things. He is in a playful mood from the time he opens his eyes until I let him know, "It's time for bed." He hates bedtime, just like every other child. He feels like he is going to miss something. He wants to play until he can no longer keep his eyes open. We wrestle every day. He lies on me and says, "Daddy, tickle me!" I always ask him who wants to be tickled, and he shouts, "Me!" He likes to say, "Daddy, smell my feet." So, I respond, "Ew, they stink. You have stinky feet." He counters, "Smell them again," as he sticks his feet in my face. We just have fun together all the time. He and I go to the mall together and shop. Sometimes I spoil him with whatever he wants because of how well he does in school. All the ladies say, "Aww, he is such a cutie." He smiles, but he doesn't realize that a few of the women are staring right at me when they say it. I don't think I'll ever have the heart to break that news to him, so I guess he'll have to learn about it right here.

Another thing that brought me true happiness was when Kiion would watch me play. After my games, I would go up to the family booth and see him running around with my teammates' children. He always wore his Buffalo jersey with my number and "Little Jones" on the back. During away games, he would have to settle for watching me on television. Right from the beginning, he enjoyed watching sports on television just as much as cartoons. He would say, "Daddy, I want to watch Buffalo," or, "I want to

217

watch Bron Bron." It was a blessed feeling knowing how much pride my son felt when he got to watch his dad on television. He would call me after games with an ecstatic voice: "Daddy, I saw you on the TV. When I get bigger, I want to be just like you. I am going to play for Buffalo just like you." It brought me so much joy knowing that he looked up to me like that. He wanted to be just like Daddy.

The one thing that terrified me was that he was watching the games live. I put it out of my mind on game day, but once in a while, the thought would sneak up on me: What if I made one wrong move and got popped and had to be carried off on a stretcher? He might remember that scene for the rest of his life. I never want to allow for a blemish on his view of me. It would also crush me if he lost respect for me because of something stupid that I did. Ideas like that scare me to death because of how much he looks up to me. I believe that's where a lot of dads lose their sons' respect. They find out their dad isn't perfect.

The following is the letter I wrote to my son before my transplant surgery, just in case.

Dear Kiion,

I love you. You and your mom are the best things that ever happened to me. You are my best friend. You bring so much joy into my life every time you run to me and jump into my arms. Every time I hear your little raspy voice scream "Daddy," I can't do anything but smile. I get chills just looking at you because you are such a happy child, and it is my most proud achievement in life that I feel like I have done my best as your father to make your world a place where you can live out your dreams. It may be difficult to believe, but you are the one person who has pushed me the most to get to the point in life where I am today. Without you, I probably wouldn't have made it into the NFL. I was rejected countless times throughout my career. People told me to my face that I wasn't good enough. Coaches overlooked me, stating that I was too slow. I always had to fight to get to where I wanted, and there was a point where I didn't know what I was going to do. I wanted to quit because I didn't know my life purpose at the time. My mission in life came clear when your mom told me that she was pregnant. I knew from that point that I had to take care of you and your mom, and that is all that has mattered to me.

Today is November 29, 2013. In a few days, your grandfather and I will be going under the knife. Your Pop Pop will be risking his life in order to save mine. We are taking part in a kidney transplant in order for me to live a healthy, productive life. If you are reading this letter, it is because I didn't make it through the surgery, so I am not here to teach you all of the things I planned. Right now, everything is in God's hands. All we can do is pray. I have some things that I need to share with you to help you become a man. I fully expect to be here to teach you these things, but if not, here they are.

1. Treat your mom with the respect and honor she deserves. She risked her life to make sure that you had the safest passage into this world. Make sure that you regularly tell Mom, and the rest of the family,

219

that you love them, and not just on holidays and birthdays. Life is short, and she won't always be there. Be a model citizen. Honor your elders and listen to their wise words. They've experienced a lot, and you can learn from their mistakes instead of making them on your own. Treat all women with respect. Treat them as the queens that they are. If you move on to have more siblings, do your best to take care of them. (Mom has my blessing to live her life as she chooses when it's my time to go, whether you agree with her decisions or not.) Put the family on your back and set the bar high for everyone to follow, just as I have tried. Put pressure on them to do better. Make sure that they get their education. Make sure that they stay out of trouble. Teach them how the world works and how cold this world can be. If you have a sister or female cousins or friends, tell them the truth about guys so that they can make the right choices when the time comes. Protect them. Be the man of the house.

2. When you are ready to do it, promise me that you will get an education. Don't just get a degree. Educate yourself. That is something that can never be taken away. It allows you to go out into this world and look people in the eyes and speak their language. Make sure you read. There is so much you can learn if you just read. (You might want to start with the book *Unbroken*, by Laura Hillenbrand. It blew me away.) Learn everything there is to learn. Don't ever stop learning, even once you are into your career. Make sure you know everything there is to know about your craft. Be the best at whatever it is that you choose to do.

3. You don't need to follow in my footsteps. Be yourself. Don't ever be scared to be different from everybody else. Remain humble, but do what you have to do to separate yourself from others. Be a leader. Don't be a follower like I was when I was young. You show signs of being a leader already with your stubborn ways, which you clearly get from your mom. I stand behind you in whatever it is that you want to do. Just promise me that if you are going to do it, make sure you go all the way. Work harder than everyone else out there. Remember that there is always someone out there working harder than you who want the same thing you want. Don't ever substitute your hard work with talent. Talent will only get you so far in this world.

4. If a sport becomes your career path, don't put extra pressure on yourself because of me. You always say that you want to be like me, and I am honored to be your role model. It would be amazing if you make it to the professional level, but less than 1 percent make it to that level. The math is scary, but that doesn't mean you can't do it. You can do whatever it is that you want, if you put your mind to it. The one thing that I ask of you is to understand the bigger picture. It's bigger than you. It always has been and it always will be. Those coaches and schools don't need you. You need them. The sport doesn't need you. You need it. It is always about business for them. It needs to be the same way for you. Handle your business first at all times. Work hard, be patient, and you will get what you deserve. Network with people at all times. Making connections and inroads with others is just as important as the opportunities you can get from

playing, and it can change your life forever. Use the sport to change your life, because they will get everything out of your body. Play the sport with the goal of owning the sport. That should be your goal in whatever business you decide to undertake. Don't ever get complacent in life. (If you don't know what "complacent" means yet, ask your teacher. And make sure you thank her afterwards.) Don't let yourself get to the point where you have played a sport and did tremendous harm to your body and soul with nothing to show for it. People love athletes. Use that to your advantage.

I love you, Kiion. I really hope that you never have to read this letter. I hope that I am here to teach you and watch you become a man. There's no ceiling for you. The only person who can get in the way of what you want is you. I say this because at three years old, I see so much of me in you. I got in my own way growing up, and I don't want you to do the same. Get out there and set the world on fire. (Not literally, son.) Whether from nearby or up above, I look forward to watching you crash through the ceiling into the skies and changing the world.

Until we meet again, Your Daddy and Big Dawg
Donald Jones

The following is the letter I wrote to my son after my transplant surgery.

Dear Son,

In the game of life, there really are no rules that you must follow. (Laws, yes; rules, not so much.) For the most part, you control the outcome of the game. You bring the ball up the court. You pass the puck. You choose to throw a knuckleball or a slider. You are the quarterback, the point guard. If you are smart, you realize that you don't need to touch the ball during every play of the game. Sometimes it's best to just put things in motion, then sit back and take notes. You're the captain of your squad. This game is full of tough decisions that you have to make every day, every play. People will count on you to make big moves. Your family members are your teammates, but this is not a team sport. This is your game. Treat your family like shoulder pads. Put your team on your back. In this card game, everyone is dealt a hand. How you play that hand is solely up to you. In this game, there will be highs and lows, as every game has. How you respond to those highs and lows is how you will be measured. If you come from the penthouse or the poor house, we are all working toward two common goals: success and preservation. At times, this game is a war. Victory will not come easily. It takes hard work every day. It takes consistency. You get one, maybe two opportunities for greatness at this game. Preparation is tremendously essential in every aspect of this game. The hard work you put into the preparation will make the end result a happy one. When preparation and opportunity meet, the end result is victory. Everything throughout this game is subject to change. When you step into the batter's box looking at a fastball and you get a curveball, what do you do? How do you adjust to change? That is how you will be remembered as a player. Despite what others will tell you, there are no moral victories in this game. There are only winners and losers. There are starters and those who ride the pine. Which

223

will you be? There is no excuse for mediocrity. Sometimes you'll get a lucky bounce or the referees will make a call in your favor. Timing is key. Sometimes you are in the right place at the right time.

The most important part of this game is to figure out how to have fun every day. It will be over before you know it. And when it's over, it's over. I hope you enjoyed the ride. What we do know is that our careers are short and when your time is up, there is nothing you can do to stop it. Don't live with regrets. The only thing worse than death is a person stuck in the past with a bag full of "what ifs." Life is a game that is to be played, not played with. The more you play with life short term, the less you enjoy long term.

The first quarter of my life has been a wild ride. It has consisted of many ups and downs. I have seen and been through a lot in my short 25 years. I have made many wrong choices in which I saw the immediate consequences. Most of the bad times came from bad choices I made, but they taught me a lot; I guess it was all part of that learning curve. The consequences of my wrong choices made me the man I am today, and without those bad times, I might not have had my good times. Often, I sit on my couch and I think back to where it all started.

Dad

At this very moment, billions of dollars are floating through the air. On any given day, countless multimillion-dollar deals are being made among sports teams, players, agents, advertisers, television stations, and clothing and beverage companies. The public is fed pieces of the puzzle throughout the year on television and the Internet (especially during Super Bowl season, when that one friend must continue his yearly tradition of updating you on how much a 30-second commercial will cost this year), but we are obviously not given the whole story — just enough to keep faith in the system and believe it is a level playing field. The business of sports goes way beyond what we see on television, in the same way that a child's education goes way beyond what happens in the classroom. For most athletes, the business side of sports starts to rear its ugly head around 12 or 13 years old, when kids are offered a deal that they notice other players on the team didn't get, like the latest pair of fresh Jordans from a coach for leaving the local team and playing for another one. As the talent of these young athletes rises, so does their value in the sport's economy. It's like a mini free agency.

Imagine a talented child. Ever since he was young, everyone has been telling him that he is better than everyone else. Coaches, parents, and friends go up to him and say, "Keep doing what you are doing, because you are better than everyone else. You have the possibility of getting out of here and making it to the pros." They put this pressure on him, and he isn't even in high school yet — and people act surprised when he messes everything up. Most of us realize that there are already shenanigans going on at the middle-school level, but very few take the time to analyze the negative effects adults with "good intentions" have.

In middle school, when kids' bodies grow in spurts, so do their skills. Suddenly, a few start to get the feeling that they're adults playing among children. The kids notice it right away, and so do their coaches. If you think coaches are intense during a close game, you haven't seen anything like one coach reacting to another trying to cherry-pick his best players. I watched coaches argue over where I would play the next season. Strangely, neither seemed the least bit interested in what I wanted, and that was when I finally understood how the prettiest girl in school must feel when guys start pounding on one another in an attempt to win her affection. And that's when the athlete's sense of entitlement is born. Just like that woman who turns all the heads, he quickly becomes accustomed to people taking care of things for him, throwing things his way. He no longer has to do schoolwork. Coaches tell him not to worry about his grades, that they've got it taken care of. Even the school administrators are in on it; that new million-dollar football field was built for more than just the graduation ceremony. Down the road, he won't even take his own SAT or ACT. They will pay someone to take it for him, someone who will be a foot shorter and possibly a different color, but the adults will have learned to look the other way if they want to keep their jobs.

These top athletes start to walk the hallways as if they can do no wrong, which is accurate, because the teachers dare not give them detention — not after they've just seen the principal high-five these guys in their varsity jackets. (Both male and female elite athletes experience major lifestyle swings, but I choose to focus on men because that is where I have firsthand experience, and where the media has chosen to shine a brighter light.) So, now these players are big men on campus. Even the local drug dealers slide them money after games, just as a college booster would. They tell them, "Stay out of these streets, because you are better than us. You are the real deal, man. You can be rich and be legit." Everyone wants to be around them because they think that they're going to be rich and famous one day. People want to clutch onto any little piece of the fame that they can get their hands on, in the same way people wrestled over Winston Churchill's discarded cigars and dug-up pieces of earth walked on by Adolf Hitler — and that was decades before eBay.

For most elite athletes, it is in their junior year of high school that they begin to be recruited by major colleges. Our athlete will be asked to visit different states and attend an assortment of camps and combines so they can start attaching numbers to his name using their standardized scales, because local statistics might be exaggerated. (Countless guys I played early ball with were on the radar of scouts only because their dads were on the coaching staff and gave them much more playing time than they deserved, which gave them inflated numbers. There were also the guys who, right after every game, went up to the girls keeping the stat books and added a few yards here and there to their plays.) The legit players at the camps and combines stand out right away. When these players post big numbers, word begins to spread nationally about this guy from a small town. That's when scholarship offers start to materialize. Schools from around the country invite these athletes to their events. Traveling there costs a decent amount of money. Many of these teens come from one-parent households, and the costs are too high; their mothers aren't working two jobs because they welcome the challenge. But that won't matter, because if they are standouts, the costs will be covered. It turns out that their moms won't have to spend any money, or they will be told, "Just pay the application fee or the lunch fee," so it at least has the appearance of being on the up and up.

All of these people from the colleges have placed the athlete on a pedestal and given him free grab bags because they want to have as many tickets in this lottery as possible. Unfortunately, the athlete is so caught up in playing the sport and thinking he is the man that he can't see what is really going on. He doesn't yet realize that half of these people have ulterior motives. He can't see how these coaches and university representatives, like dirty politicians, are positioning themselves for potential business down the road.

The student's recruiting trail is now massive. Everywhere he or she goes, they being interviewed. The biggest magazines and websites related to college ball have him ranked among the top players in the country. His high school is suddenly decorated with his latest reviews. His confidence is at an all-time high. He has the opportunity to choose whatever school in the country he wants to attend. But first, he has to make his official visits.

When he arrives at these schools, the coaches tell him he's the next Peyton Manning or Richard Sherman. They sell him on the school. They tell him how the university will position him to be great and make sure he moves on to the next level. After they pump him up to think he's a rock star, the women enter the picture with instructions to seal the deal. The ladies take him to clubs, fraternities, and private parties where he calls the shots. The seed is planted, and he starts to think to himself, *if this is what college is like in one weekend, I'll be a legend in months. I'm definitely coming here.*

One major problem. His mom needs some overdue bills paid. One of the contender colleges arranges to have them taken care of. They set the payments up through someone else so that it doesn't appear on their books, just like the housing costs of those college women who showed him a good time. He accepts it because they assure him everyone's doing it and there's no way to get caught. Now he has sold his soul. He feels that if they pulled out all the stops for him, they must really need him. He gets it in his mind that he's going to that first recruiting school because there's no way that anyone could top the wild nights they gave him a taste of. But he still visits all the rest of the schools he's allowed to, because he has reached a new plateau in life, and that taste of the VIP lifestyle lingers.

The coaches have now sold themselves, and it is time for the student to declare his school of choice. He has a big event set up to announce where he will be attending. ESPN is showing his announcement live on television. It feels as if everyone is waiting to hear his decision. That day comes, and he announces that he is going to attend the school that has the best program. He never took into account anything that had to do with his actual education, because he couldn't get those college girls out of his mind. He starts thinking, "I can always come back and get my education." And once he gets his fill of the party scene, he is going to the NFL the first chance he gets.

The next summer, he arrives at his chosen school. The first twist he notices is that the coaches have changed. They are not the same people who recruited him. He thought they were the best of friends, but now that they have him on campus, it's a different story. Some of the coaches are even harder on him than on the other players because he was such a high recruit. They say to him, "You're not as good as you think you are. You'd better step your game up. This ain't high school, son." Like in the military, once you sign on that dotted line, they've got you, and you jump when they say jump.

The next thing he notices is that everyone on the team was a high recruit. He is suddenly just another guy on a team full of All-Americans. For the first time in his life, he feels average, which really messes with his head. Now he has to work his tail off in order to earn a starting spot. The problem is that he has never had to work for anything in his life; it all came easily. He doesn't know what it is like to have to work that hard for something. The coaches will only play the guys who work the hardest and put the team in the best position to win. It's all business for them, as they are trying to win in order to get a new contract from the school or move up to the professional level. They already make millions, but now they are after the only thing more important than money at their level: power.

Now he is in a dogfight for a starting spot. The coaches end up giving someone else the spot. They approach him and say, "You're not ready for this stage yet, and we are going to redshirt you." The only thing he gets to do in his first year is practice. All these years, he has been the man, and now he won't even suit up for a single game that season. They made him feel like he was a clear-cut starter coming in. Now he feels like a nobody on the team. He is on the other side of the country by himself. Mom can't help him. He'll have to do this on his own. He'll have to tell his best friends back home to cancel that road trip to homecoming.

The next year comes, and the coaches bring in another All-American out of high school. That player ends up starting over him, as well. Now he feels betrayed. He begins slacking off in the classroom. He doesn't really care about team meetings, because he feels he will never play. He has gone so long with that sense of entitlement that he cannot handle this swing.

When he was recruited, he thought they needed him. Now he sees that they don't.

The coaches decide to go after more All-Americans out of high school at his position. They don't feel he has panned out to be the player they had hoped. They only have a certain number of scholarships, and now the business kicks in. The coaches begin private talks about guys they want to phase out of the team. His name comes up. "He is never going to play. He isn't strong enough. He's too slow. He has been slacking off in all his classes. He just doesn't have it. We need more talent at his position. What do we want to do with him? We have to add someone, but we don't have room." They know that they can find a way to get him off scholarship. They set up 5 a.m. practices to see who will be late. Any guy who is late is off the team. He ends up late. Now he loses his scholarship and has to go back home. They never mentioned that rule about being late, but it was hidden somewhere in a contract that he signed. He didn't know that they could take away his scholarship. He thought it was a guarantee for all four years. The loss of his scholarship frees the coaches to bring in someone else. The business of college sports has just chewed him up and spit him out.

Things like this happen all the time. As athletes, we get so caught up in ourselves that we never see the bigger picture. We get this sense of entitlement and invincibility. We believe that these schools or teams need us. The truth is that we need them. Everything on their end is business. They don't stop to think about your family or the things you have going on back home. If you can't help that team win, you will be sent packing.

Beginning at the youngest levels, parents are pouring billions into their children in the hopes that they will become stars, investing early to gain an advantage in this horse race. They are all hoping that their child will be the next LeBron. They will do whatever it takes to ensure that he has the best opportunities to make it in the sports world. Most parents today are aware of how difficult it is to make it to the professional level. But just as with the lottery, statistics don't matter, because they can all point to someone they know or have met who beat the odds — and if it happened for him, why not for us?

Despite the bias we all have when it comes to our children, let's go over the numbers, just so things are concrete. Less than 1 percent of teens playing a high-school sport have a legitimate shot at making it pro. Only a fraction of that 1 percent will ever suit up for a game in the major leagues. And only a fraction of that number will get to play in enough seasons to be able to label it a career.

We are seeing more and more parents force their children to play sports that they don't like. Parents do this because they think their child can be the best, or because they are living vicariously through him. They need to take the time to pay attention to the signs their child gives of whether he likes the sport or not. They cannot force him to play. Doing so can ultimately ruin their relationship with their child, or that child's mentality.

Grades must come before anything else. This should be engraved into a child's head from day one all the way through college. That child can't make it anywhere without good grades, no matter how talented he is.

Coaches will not take a chance on someone who has no work ethic, and grades are the first sign of not having what it takes.

As we move up into the high-school ranks, we start to see the big business on the institutional side. We see high-school coaches recruit children at very young ages. These (mostly private) schools will do anything to get your child to come. They will package-deal another child in order to get the one they really want. The other child will never get the recognition that he feels he deserves. They will offer a parent something in return for sending their child to that school. Understand that if you partake in any of these illegal activities, that school now has leverage. They own you.

Once in high school, the big business becomes even more prevalent. Now that child has a chance at becoming a star athlete. Billions of dollars are poured into camps and combines around the world every year in the hopes that he or she will earn that golden ticket, a free ride to college. Parents must understand that it is essential for their child to attend these events in order to get the necessary exposure. Just realize that there are certain rules.

Athletes in high school rarely understand the bigger picture. They believe they are way better than they are. This stems from years of being pushed through levels of school and life because they may become stars. Because athletes are ushered through and treated like kings, they never really take the time to excel at anything except sports. The best professionals in the world are able to juggle sports with education and business. If you don't get your education, you will be lost. You probably won't make it into the college that you want to make it into. If you pay attention, you will notice that each year, it is getting harder and harder to get into college.

It is not the coaches' job to make sure your child makes it to the professional level. It is their job to win games and put people in the seats of their stadium, even if they burn out his arm or do irreparable damage to his knees. That's how they make their money and the school's money. It is way bigger than your child. It's big business. It's your and your child's job to make sure that he graduates. It's your job to make sure that he doesn't just graduate, but truly educates himself. It's your job to make sure that he stays out of trouble.

The first part of the business he will go through is the sports agent. That is a separate business within the business. Agents and financial advisers look at him the same way a coach or owner does. He can help them make money. If they feel that he can't make them money, most of them won't want any part of him. Understand that once he signs with them, they should work for him and not the other way around. They can talk collectively about things, but ultimately, he calls the shots. He must pay attention to his money and what is going on with it. Don't let his agents or advisers talk him into a business transaction that he knows nothing about. The reason he doesn't know anything about business is that he never learned anything but football in school. Agents and financial advisers are very smart. They have the knowledge and connections to rip him out of millions of dollars. It has happened to many players, and it will happen to him if he is not smart and attentive.

The next part of this business is the coaches and owners. As a player, he will play with heart and passion. He will be very loyal to the sport and the team he plays for. But the coaches and owners will never be loyal to him. They won't care who he is or who he was. Players fuel the various leagues, institutions, and organizations. The leagues need the players collectively to help them make money. But as an individual, they don't need him. They coach and own with their business minds. If he can't help that team win and make more money, then he is gone. They don't care about his family or his situation at home. It is his job to educate himself and handle his money right.

Most players don't walk away from the game of their own will. They are usually forced out after a short time because of injury or diminishing skill. He needs to network with people while he is in the game. He should be networking from high school all the way through the professional level. That NFL, NBA, MLB, NHL, or any other shield speaks volumes behind his name. Networking can set him up to make more money later than he ever did playing the sport. His sports legacy is one thing, but what will his life legacy be? Will he be able to maintain the lifestyle he had while playing after he is done?

He will put his body through vast amounts of stress playing the sport. He will go through a lot of injuries and pain. It would be a shame if he did all that for nothing. It would be a shame if he had nothing to show for it in the end.

Made in the USA
San Bernardino, CA
09 June 2016